C000221799

Stripping It ___

Billy Dixon

Gullion Media Limited

This paperback edition published in 2011 by
Gullion Media Limited, c/o 11 Slieve Crescent, Dromintee,
Newry, Co. Down, BT35 8UF, Northern Ireland.

First published in UK by Gullion Media Limited, 2011.

Edited by George J. Kingsnorth
Proof Readers: Jeff Marshall & Molly Dixon

www.gullionmedia.com
www.billydixon.co.uk

A CIP catalogue record for this book is
available from the British Library

ISBN 978-0-9560403-3-6

Contents

1.   Introduction

If all of our technologies and infrastructures were taken away from us and we had to revert to surviving by our instincts, I wonder how many of us could cope? It's a question that has been addressed by numerous writers, disaster films and television programmes – all of which would suggest that we would revert to a primitive state and that it would be the survival of the fittest.

So does that primitive instinct lie dormant within us all? The answer is probably, according to the experts. Social studies conducted on deprived areas, within America and Britain where there were high levels of unemployment, showed a greater incidence of crimes such as burglary, muggings and other types of theft. Gang culture was also more prevalent in these areas and many young people had themselves *badged* with their tribal colours.

Where there is no work and very little hope people are more likely to revert to hunter-gather behaviour. This can manifest itself in theft, which by its very nature is predatory, and the marking of territory, which is in essence tribal. These actions may fly in the face of our definition of a civilised society but in truth are often the result of a forgotten class of people who are simply trying to survive and as a result do not have the same value set as the rest of us.

It has been generally accepted that when faced with stressful situations, we tend to revert to our primitive instincts. Quite often these instincts will determine our reactions both physically and mentally and unless we can understand and start to control them then we are often at a disadvantage.

Why, when I go into a room of strangers do I feel uncomfortable, nervous, and shy? The answer is very simple; my primitive survival instinct is on high alert. I don't know these people, I could be attacked, my safety might be under threat and I am walking into the unknown. As a result my body goes into fight or flight mode, hence the nervous stomach, the increased heartbeat and the general feeling of unease. In other words how I am feeling is natural.

Despite how I feel I know that I cannot just turn and run, or lash out and attack the nearest person. If I am to be accepted and to progress in my career I must handle my emotions and control my natural instincts.

The important thing to remember is that how I feel is natural; it is not me being inadequate or inferior, it's just that my instincts are telling me I could be under threat. To have confidence in such a situation is not something that most people would feel naturally, it is something that has to be learnt and developed over time.

When we are certain about something then we are confident, and when we are not certain about something we are not confident. In stressful situations we tend to revert to a primitive state with all the associated symptoms and reactions. This often results in a drop in confidence, which can put the individual at a real disadvantage.

However, if we can develop more self-confidence this will help us deal with uncertainty much better. Now I hear you asking — what is the difference between confidence and self-confidence?

- Confidence is being certain about an outcome or a result.

- Personal/self-confidence is having confidence in yourself.

Self-confidence does not necessarily imply 'self-belief' or a belief in your ability to succeed. There are those who may not be good at a particular sport or activity but still appear and act with confidence, because they have no real interest in the activity or its outcome and have accepted that they cannot be good at everything.

Dwelling upon the consequences of failure and the negative reaction of others can reduce personal-confidence and as a result affect performance. However, if we can focus upon the processes involved in the activity and the enjoyment that that brings then we are more likely to succeed and build personal-confidence. This simple solution will help an individual build belief in their abilities and therefore improve personal-confidence.

And that is why this book was written, to give you, the reader, a greater understanding about the basic elements of personal-confidence and how these are related to our natural instincts, our belief system, and in some cases our physiology. It does not go into fluffy concepts and theories, nor does it go into the world of psycho-babble that is found in so many self-help books today. This is a practical manual that gives you a series of tools and ideas to improve your personal confidence. Some readers may use all the advice given, whereas other may only need to use part of it.

As someone who had very little personal-confidence and poor self-esteem for most of my life, I have read every self-help book I could find, in fact my garage is full of them. I tried my very best to embrace the ideas and concepts within many of these publications, but when I kept failing to meet their criteria or started to backslide, I felt worse and less confident than I did before I started. When I looked into the claims made by some of these authors, I discovered that many of their concepts were not validated by any research and on several cases the stated study had not even taken place or was fraudulent.

That is why the advice in this book has been based, as far as possible, upon the latest validated research in the disciplines of psychology and neuro-science. I have used all of the principles included to improve my own personal confidence and have been privileged to witness positive changes in other people's lives who have also applied them. However, please remember, nothing is perfect, no book, self-help programme or guru can have all of the answers, but perhaps this publication will help you find a few.

2 Who I am

It has taken me a long time to write this book, or should I say it has taken me years to take the time to sit down and write this book. For years, I have had the ideas swimming around in my head but did not think what I had to say was important or useful enough for others to want to read it.

Over the years, more and more people attending my talks ask "Have you written a book"? And my answer was always "I'm in the process of writing one". Of course, as a confirmed procrastinator, I never got around to doing it and if truth be told I did not believe I could.

The words on these pages represent a massive journey for me — from the angry young man who wanted to hit out at the world, to the angry old man who wants to change the world. This journey has taught me much, the baseness of man: the importance of relationships, the hollowness of possessions, the danger of closed minds, the ease of manipulation, the failure of education, the curse of extremisms and the power of love.

I am not an idealist or any other kind of "ist" and no-where on this journey has the meaning of life or any other great revelations been given to me. I realise that no-one is, or ever will be perfect, and that life is unpredictable.

There are a few who have found fulfilment but many, many more who are looking for it. There are self-appointed gurus who claim to have the answers but really have not understood the question.

There is no way I can be called a guru. Bald — yes but not a guru. In my own mind I am a teacher, someone who gives others the tools and knowledge to challenge, change and progress in life. My methods are simple and practical, and are based upon real research, experience and logic rather than trendy psycho-babble.

Am I a confident man, who is happy with his lot, and who is living a fulfilled life? The truth is that I have good days and bad days like most people. However, the difference between today and several years ago is that I have much more control and understanding over the psychological aspects of my life, which in turn allows me to be happier, more positive and more confident.

My story is similar, I'm sure, to many other authors (see I am calling myself an author now) and non-authors. Someday, perhaps, I will write a full account of the life and times of Billy Dixon but for the time being here is a condensed version of my journey to date.

In summary then:

- Mother's name Jean, father's name Norman, and sister's name Maureen.

- Lived in a fabulous rural community outside

Markethill in South Armagh.

- Father died when I was twelve years old, the result of a brain tumour and nine years of extreme suffering.

- Raised in a house with no running water, no electricity and with a fabulous outdoor toilet which I had to empty every Saturday.

- Father's family had a liking for hard drinking, womanising and fighting.

- My sister and I enjoyed an idyllic childhood (apart from the cold) and were never aware of the poverty.

- I was written off, educationally, at a very early age and labelled as slow.

- Failed everything up until the age of sixteen but had a ball doing it.

- Was inspired by a teacher called Peggy Greer who made rejects like me feel special. Peggy really did change people's lives.

- To everyone's surprise I ended up going to university and over the years got qualifications in business studies, marketing and psychology.

- Decided I wanted to follow in Peggy Greer's footsteps and trained as a teacher.

- Had the privilege of teaching in a further education college for twenty-two years. Hopefully, I changed a few lives during that time.

- Was motivated by the students but disillusioned by

the internal politics of the college.

- Started jumping out of airplanes in 1984 and have since completed over 3,000 skydives. During this time I have had three malfunctions, all of which were my own fault – great examples of how dangerous familiarity and complacency are.

- Took a career break in 1986 to get my mojo back and to study Marketing at John Moore in Liverpool.

- Was inspired by a lateral thinker and lecturer Dr Peter Williamson who helped me regain my enthusiasm for education.

- Won the fittest man in the world competition and had to break the world record in gym tests to do it

- Took up Aikido and was taught by a wonderful old gentleman and second world war veteran, Charlie Simms. With Charlie's guidance I got my black belt and instructor's license.

- Left teaching to work for myself in 1998. It felt very scary knowing that I had to generate my own income rather than have the security of a regular teacher's salary.

- The year I left teaching to start my own business I also discovered that I was severely dyslexic. This came as a complete surprise as I just thought that I was stupid.

- The most important things in my life are my two children, Molly and Theo, both of whom I love to bits.

- I love what I do, have lots of fun, meet interesting people and I get paid for it.

My life can be mapped out very easily: under achiever, felt inadequate, needed to be accepted, had no confidence, got inspired, went to the extremes to prove himself, had a lucky break, realised there was a lot more like him, now shares what he learnt and teaches others.

My story is no more remarkable than many others, but it has helped make me the person I am today. I know I owe a lot to the genes passed on to me by my parents and there are things that I can never change about myself. It is the acceptance of me the person that is Billy Dixon and the management of my strengths and weaknesses that has allowed me to develop and grow as an individual.

I now know that adversity can make some people stronger but it can also destroy others.

In the early 1970s a huge car bomb was left in the village outside the home my mother, sister and I lived in. We were unable to get out of the building so we sheltered in a back room with several other people. When the bomb exploded, the lights went out and part of the wall came in around us. There was panic and screaming in this dark tomb during the night. Some were trying to claw their way out through the blocked door and two individuals were just lying in shock. Then my mother took control, this small shy women became a tower of strength for everyone spreading calm, making sure no-one was injured and guiding us all to safety.

My mother is a great example of someone with hidden

depths and strengths that only seemed to surface in a crisis. She nursed an invalided husband while bringing up two young children. She was widowed at a very young age. Provided for and financed her two children through further and higher education. Had her home destroyed by bombs on several occasions and had to start again.

Why is it that some people only seem to shine when there is a crisis? The answer is to do with self-esteem and confidence. A confident person has a good level of self-awareness and feels comfortable using their talents and abilities. A person without confidence and who has poor self-esteem and low levels of self-awareness are inclined to downplay or even hide their talents and abilities.

Many of the students I taught had their self-belief knocked out of them because of a flawed educational system. When they arrived to me they had been labelled failures, their self-esteem was often non-existent, they believed they were second-class and many harboured anger and resentment. My job was simple, give them subject knowledge but more importantly, I felt, I had to help them get their confidence and self-respect back again.

For someone that suffered from low self-esteem and confidence, working with the students was as much a journey of self-discovery for me as it was for them. We learnt together, developed together and succeeded together. It was in this environment that I became interested in personal development and many of the principles that I use in this book were developed in the classrooms of Portadown Technical College.

In the years since then I have witnessed some people quit in the sight of victory because they subconsciously did not believe they deserved it. I have watched individuals born with a God given talent self-destruct and fail while others with no talent at all became hugely successful. Could I have helped any of these people? Possibly — but only if they wanted help.

And it is in that last line we come to the crux of the matter. There is no one-size-fits-all in developing personal confidence. There are things in this book that may be of use to you and other parts that you may not be able to relate to, that is not the real issue. What is really important is that you want to develop and improve your personal confidence. If that is the case then you will seek out and pick what is useful for you from a number of sources, be they books, the web, courses or other people.

3 Clearing the ground.

Being successful

What I have realised is that success is not guaranteed but neither is it a mystery. The bookshelves are full of publications written by some who tell us how to become successful and others who tell us how they became successful.

I believe that success (whatever that means to you) lies within us all. It may be born out of adversity or privilege. It is not restricted to the academic elite or those with the greatest brainpower. Age and health may affect our physical abilities but in most cases do not prevent us from being successful.

Success, even in sport, is born and nurtured in our thought processes. Self-esteem and confidence feed and strengthen this desire so that obstacles and setbacks are seen as challenges to be overcome and learned from.

Success therefore is a mind set that has to be developed and maintained until it becomes part of our very being. History is full of well-known individuals whose mental strength carried them through. One of my favourites is the little known Bessie Coleman.

Bessie was an aviator in the 1920s who built a reputation for being one of the best barnstorming (stunt) pilots of her generation. Born in the southern states of America, she was brought up in poverty and was witness to extreme racism.

She developed her fascination for flying at a young age. She worked in the cotton fields and saved as much money as she could to pay for flying lessons. She then went around America to various flying schools but none would teach her how to fly because of the colour of her skin. Eventually she went to France to get her pilot's licence where race was not such an issue.

Back in America, Bessie started barnstorming and soon became a crowd favourite, drawing in thousands of people to see her fly. Within no time, the air show authorities were asking her to organise shows on their behalf. She agreed but conditionally. She insisted that there would be no segregation of the crowd and all peoples — no matter what their race, creed or skin colour — should be allowed to sit together. The authorities agreed and in this way Bessie had helped towards sowing the seeds of equality for all men.

Later Bessie applied for her flying instructor's licence, but again the American flying schools refused to let her do the course, so she went back to France. She returned to America a fully qualified flying instructor and taught everyone no matter what their background, race, or religion. Bessie Coleman was non-discriminate, giving all she encountered equal opportunity.

Unfortunately, she came to an untimely end while teaching her engineer how to fly. In an open cockpit aircraft, she leant over her engineers shoulder to give instructions as he flipped the plane over. Bessie accidentally fell to her death as she had not been strapped in. A sad end to a great individual.

Bessie Coleman, though not familiar to many people today, left behind a profound statement that each one of us should read and reflect upon.

"This is who I am; I am someone who wants to make a difference in the world that I live in".

We all can make a difference but first we have to want to. There are those who will just accept the status quo and drift through life, and then there are others who are proactive and want to create a legacy. To make a difference we have to instil confidence in others and to do that we have to understand ourselves. Bessie Coleman was driven by the passion for flying and the passion for equality, this gave her the resilience and the confidence to persuade others to adopt her ideals. Without this passion Bessie would not have had the mental toughness to overcome so many obstacles. Her personal belief and confidence inspired others to change and this is where we start *our* journey of self-improvement.

Passion — the first element of success.

The world would be a much sadder place without passion. It has built cities, created great works of art, been responsible for incredible acts of kindness and written heart rendering love stories. However, it can also be incredibly destructive if allied to extreme or distorted belief systems.

History is littered with the result of misguided passion where lives have been destroyed. No matter how we look at it passion is a huge motivator, and if embraced can be a very positive force.

Success, however we decide to measure it, is driven by passion. It overrides mental ability, talent, money and influence. Without it no matter how gifted an individual is, without passion success is unachievable.

Passion creates a mental toughness and a resilience that will help overcome obstacles, hard times, setbacks, self-doubt and even failure. It creates focus, direction and enthusiasm.

Without it individuals tend to be less enthusiastic, are more inclined to give up easily, are less persistent and seldom have real belief in what they are doing.

Essentially there are two types of passion:

- **Love**: the passion of love is very powerful, it draws us to it, and we want to be part of it. Love tends to be singular; we love a person, a cause, music, art, a sport and so on. Love becomes part of our identity and may even be a reflection of our status within society. In terms of motivation love is hugely influential and leaders must always consider it when working with their teams.

- **Hate**: the passion of hate is also very powerful. History is full of leaders who have used hate to motivate their followers. Hate can create feelings of injustice, victimisation, isolation, anger and revenge.

Billy Dixon

It can unite people under a common banner and drive them to achieve extraordinary results.

Of course, some unscrupulous leaders have used both of these passions for their own selfish and sometimes evil agendas. However, used properly, love and hate are the cornerstones of motivation for any leader and their followers.

For individuals who would like to develop themselves on a personal level, the starting point is always passion. Bessie Coleman for example, loved flying but hated racism — and it was these two passions that carried her through the hard times and the inevitable periods of self-doubt.

Question:
What are your love passions?

You notice I say passions not passion. Most of us will have more than one passion. We may have a passion for the well-being of our children; we may have a passion for music, or a sport, our career, our business or even a hobby.

What are the things in life that you really love and affect you on an emotional level?

Make your list love passions:

What are your hate passions?

What are the things in life that really irritate you and affect you on an emotional level?

Make your list hate passions:

With each list rank your passions in chronological order

where "No. 1" is the most passionate.

You now have two lists that indicate your motivational drivers, knowing these will help give you a greater understanding of what drives you. Instinctively you will be drawn to those things that you love and you will tend to avoid those things that you hate.

Doing something we love is a joy and a great confidence booster. However, there are times we must face the things we hate. Bessie Coleman hated racism yet she confronted it and tried to change people's attitudes. Doing something you hate may be uncomfortable but it is also a great confidence booster if you are able to confront and overcome your demons.

Hate is a powerful driver, providing you can harness it and use it constructively. Sports coaches have always used it as a way to motivate their athletics and teams. However, it must be controlled, otherwise it can be very damaging and destructive. Doing something we hate in a controlled manner is a great confidence booster

James is a motivational speaker who enjoys the buzz of performing on stage, his presentations are hugely popular and he regularly receives an abundance of accolades. At every one of his talks over the last ten years he is always asked, "Do you have a book?" James has always answered; "I'm in the process of writing one and it will be published shortly."

Now, James knows that there is a demand for his material in book form. He genuinely wants to write one, knows what he wants to put into it, and has started planning and writing on numerous occasions. Why has he still not completed his book? Well let's have a look at his motivational drivers.

James's Love passions:

- Performing: gives him immediate feedback and an adrenal rush.

- Escape: allows him to escape the mundane routine of day-to-day living.

- Attention: makes him the centre of attention and gets him lots of praise.

- Self-expression: enables his views to be taken seriously by influential individuals.

James's Hate passions:

- Being ordered around: he dislikes being told what to do, and he prefers to be asked.

- Routine: he dislikes routine but enjoys doing things on impulse.

- Confined spaces: he dislikes being in confined spaces and prefers open environments.

- Administration: he dislikes being bogged down by administrative paperwork but prefers to get on with the job of presenting.

- Isolation: he dislikes being isolated for long periods of time.

James does not have the will to sit down and routinely write his book as long as he is getting the recognition and adulation from his performances. He is passionate about his presentations but does not have the passion to sit down and write his book.

Without passion we tend to be uncommitted and only pay lip service to the job or task at hand. This is one of the reasons so many people are unhappy in their work. Without passion there is no connection and as a result people have no real purpose.

Purpose — the second element of success.

Purpose gives an individual direction in their life, helps them maintain commitment and often gives their life meaning.

We all know people who hate their jobs and live for the weekends and holidays or others who are unfortunate to be unemployed and have resigned themselves to their circumstances. The lack of purpose in their lives often results in a hollow shell deprived of hope.

What creates purpose? A big question but one with a simple answer. Passion creates purpose! Without passion there can be no purpose and passion without purpose can never be fulfilled, the two are interlinked.

Now, I know that there are those who would claim that we have only one purpose in life, this is something that I disagree with fundamentally. In my opinion, I believe we all

Billy Dixon

can have numerous purposes throughout our lifetime.

Until I met Peggy Green I was drifting through life without any real meaning or purpose and heading for a dead end job. Her enthusiasm and dedication sparked something in me and my classmates. All of a sudden things started to make sense.

I knew at that stage that I wanted to teach, to try and change the lives of young people who did not have the best start in life. This I saw as my purpose.

Fitness and health have always been a big passion of mine and, after I had settled into teaching, I became more serious about my physical training and decided to compete to the best of my ability. This I saw as a second purpose.

When I look at my life and everything I have done, I would say I have been passionate about many things. In turn, these passions gave me the purpose to get involved in these two activities.

Of course, there are tasks I no longer feel passionate about and have become less and less involved with. In other words, I have lost my passion and, subsequently, lost my purpose.

I have a real purpose in:

Make a list of those areas in your life where you believe you have a real purpose.

Focus — the third element of success.

Focus is the practical part of success; it brings passion and purpose together to get things done. 'Passion' is the motivator; 'Purpose' is what we want to do; and 'Focus' is what we have to do to achieve it.

There may be times when we have to focus on doing things that we do not really enjoy in order to achieve our purpose. There are some sports stars that enjoy competing but dislike the training and many business executives relish their position but dislike the long hours spent travelling.

Being focused includes everything that needs to be done in order to achieve our purpose, including the good and the bad — the dull, the exciting, the clean and the dirty.

History is full of examples of how the loss of focus and attention to detail can destroy success. Practically every empire has fallen because the powers that be, lost focus and forgot what their original purpose was. I have personally witnessed businesses, individuals and sport teams destroy their success by neglecting the little things that got them to where they were in the first place.

The Irish rugby team had just scored a try and were leading England in the first match the two teams had played at Croke Park, the home of the GAA. It was the last few minutes of the game and if Ireland could prevent the English from scoring they would not only record a famous victory at this great stadium but they were also in line to win a grand slam.

The Irish were still celebrating the try they had just scored and were not concentrating on the continuation of the game. The English burst through the Irish defence, scored a try and won the match in the dying seconds. This simple loss of focus by the Irish team lost them the match and the Grand Slam.

Several years ago, I was coaching a young journalist on visual media projection for the BBC. She looked good, sounded good and had a real instinct on how to project herself to the camera. With her talent as a journalist and her ability before the camera, she fulfilled her lifetime ambition and was given the anchor spot on a regional TV news station.

For several years everything was going well, then she started taking her position for granted and become very casual in her approach to her appearance and interviews, often not even taken the time to be briefed about the interviewees. It was only a matter of time before she was replaced and was returned to the field as a roving reporter.

Unfortunately, this scenario is all too common throughout all walks of life. Individuals and organisations can be very focused on achieving something, but relax, and become distracted once they reach their aim.

In some circles this is referred to as "black belt syndrome." The martial artist focuses all of their efforts on achieving the rank of first Dan black belt. After years of commitment and sacrifice they finally achieve their aim, with all the accolades and respect that goes with it. Then having put all the effort and work into reaching this level they quit, leaving the coaching team scratching their heads in puzzlement. The reason for this behaviour is a very simple one; the martial artist focused everything on achieving their black belt but had not thought about what they were going to do once they received it.

To be focused one must always have something to aim for. A politician may be focused on becoming party leader, if they achieve that, then they must focus on taking the party forward to win a majority at the next election. If they achieve that, then they must focus on taking over the reins of power and so on.

In other words focus should be staged

Think of the young archer who dreams of winning a gold medal at the Olympic games. To get to that level they have to:

- Win their club championship.

- Win their county championship.

- Win national competitions.

- Qualify to represent their country.

- Compete at international meets.

- Qualify for the Olympic games.

- Win a gold medal.

Billy Dixon

This young archer needs to completely focus only on the next stage. By thinking too far ahead there is a real danger of complacency and loss of form. However, once one level has been achieved then the focus is instantly moved to the next target.

Exercise:

- What is your overall aim or purpose?

- What landmarks do you need to reach to achieve this?

- Focus all of your efforts on achieving the first landmark.

- Once you have achieved the first landmark, focus on the next one.

It is really important that you only focus on one stage at a time and not become distracted by the subsequent stages. Always remember the basics, as these are the foundation of your success.

Yehudi Menuhin, considered to be one of the greatest violin players of all time, practiced the basic musical scales for several hours every day. This discipline and mastery of the basics was something he retained until the end of his career.

If we go back to the young archer, he will only be successful if he retains his focus upon the basics, so no matter what his objective he must always remember;

- He has to hit a target seventy-five meters away. The centre of that target is the focus but a lot of preparation and processes have to be gone through to take the shot.

- The mind has to be in the right place.

- The correct equipment has to be chosen and in good working order.

- All distractions have to be eliminated before the shot is taken.

- A pre-shot routine needs to be gone through.

- All technical aspects for taking the shot must be adhered to.

- The arrow is released.

- The result will be monitored and adjustments made for the next shot.

- If he looses his focus on any of these stages then his progress is halted.

Exercise:

- What are the basics required in your chosen field?

- How can you improve these?

To achieve something we have to work out the processes of how to get there. Because we live in such a dynamic environment it is important that those processes have a degree of flexibility attached to them to respond to changing conditions.

All successful people have focus and will retain that focus no matter what is going on around them. It is this single-minded approach that sets them apart from the rest. This type of mind-set is essential for success but it does come at a price. To be so single-minded requires sacrifice; and to be frank there are some who are just not prepared to pay that price.

Types of focus:

- **Strategic focus.** This individual knows exactly what they want to achieve, they can visualise the result and the rewards. They can communicate their aim with great enthusiasm and motivate everyone around them. However, they may not be that practical in how to get there and will need help with the planning and development stages.

- **Tactical focus.** This individual is not an original thinker and will get their objective from an outside source such as the strategic thinker. Once they have this they will become totally focused in working out how to get there. Every step of the journey will be set out in detailed plans.

- **Instinctive focus.** These individuals know what they want to achieve but find it very difficult to stick to plans and processes. They tend to play everything through the seat of their pants, reacting to situations as they arise. They are very good at spotting opportunities and taking advantage of them and will be creative in their analysis and thinking.

- **Practical focus.** These individuals need to be told what to do but once given the target will not quit until they achieve it. They are very practical in everything they do and tend to dismiss fancy concepts and theories. No project or job can be completed without the single-minded determination of this group, they are hugely important, but unfortunately often undervalued.

Loss of focus.

There are many reasons why we lose focus and the majority of these, although avoidable, creep up and take us off track gradually.

- **Distractions.** We can be distracted by family, friends, television, alcohol, drugs and even with what is happening in the news.

- **Fatigue.** Overwork and stress will eventually take their toll affecting an individual emotionally and physically, making rational decisions more difficult.

- **Disillusionment.** Many people start off with high ideals only to have them shattered by unscrupulous and ruthless individuals.

- **Success.** This does bring rewards and it is a great confidence booster. However, it can also bring with it contentment and a loss of hunger. There are many who have taken their success for granted and ended up losing it.

- **Failure.** Losing can make some people feel dejected, reducing their confidence and self-esteem. If these feelings are not handled properly, there is a greater danger of giving up.

- **Adulation.** Praise is good providing it is taken in context, but there are some who believe the hype and take it too seriously. Sadly many of these people get distracted and focus on the adulation rather than what they should be doing.

- **Criticism.** How we handle criticism, is often determined by our levels of self-esteem. For some being criticised destroys their personal confidence, they lose focus and give up. Others are fired up by criticism and become more focused. Then there are some who focus on addressing the criticism and lose sight of what it was they were trying to achieve.

This is by no means a comprehensive list of all the things that cause loss of focus and I am sure that there are many more that I have not thought about. However, the really important question is: how do we retain focus when the pressure is on and things are not going our way?

Maintaining focus.

- **Personal discipline.** This is without doubt the most

important element of focus. Be disciplined in everything that you do and that includes taking time off to spend time with family and friends or doing something that you enjoy.

- **Revert to the basics.** Always make a point of doing the basics right. In times of stress this often refocuses the mind.

- **Do your job.** Too many people only see the win but forget about how they are going to achieve it. Always focus on the processes and simply do your job.

- **Do a commentary.** If you find yourself being distracted, talk to yourself and do a commentary on what you are doing and what is going on around you. This is a great way of bringing the mind back to what you should be doing.

- **Be answerable to someone.** Working with a friend or colleague who will monitor your efforts and progress and provide honest feedback is worth considering. They can help you maintain discipline, set deadlines, review quality and keep you on track.

Summary.

- Passion is the great motivator, if we love something or hate something we are more inclined to go the extra mile.

- Passion creates a mental toughness and resilience.

- Passion creates purpose.

- Purpose gives direction, helps maintain commitment and often gives life meaning.

- We can have more than one purpose.

- Passion may motivate us and give us purpose. Purpose may give us direction. But we will never achieve our goals if we don't have focus.

- Focus needs to be staged if we are to have continued success rather than have a one-hit wonder.

- There are many ways of loosing focus so therefore learning how to retain or regain it is crucial.

4   Personal Confidence

Contrary to what some self-help expert's claim, confidence has very little to do with our genetic make-up. Confidence is something we develop and learn from our experiences throughout our lives. It tends to be transient and may change on a daily basis depending upon our mood and the circumstances that we find ourselves in. It may not be real, but rather an act that creates a perception.

Developing personal confidence is a decision, but it is not one that everyone is prepared to make. For some there are lots of benefits gained from not having confidence.

Benefits of not having confidence:

- Receive lots of attention and encouragement.

- No one sees them as a threat.

- Can shirk responsibility.

- Do not have to try to hard, as they are not expected to succeed.

- Do not feel guilty when they fail.

- Very little expected off them by others.

- Always have an excuse for poor behaviour.

Billy Dixon

- Can pass the blame on to others.

So as you can see, lack of confidence does have its advantages. It does provide some individuals with a comfort zone that they are reluctant to step out off.

However, the benefits of having personal confidence by far outweigh the advantages of not having it; yet it should be remembered that it is something that has to be developed and worked on, it does not just happen. Building personal confidence therefore is a choice.

Real confidence is not based in bravado. In fact, the most confident people tend to be humble individuals who are not scared of making mistakes or asking for help.

On some courses I have been on, the facilitator (this is not what I would like to call them) have instructed us to get rid of self doubt, claiming that self-doubt has no part of a confident, successful, person's mind-set. The fact is, self-doubt is natural and if controlled, can be quite healthy, it makes individuals examine their talents and ability's while looking for ways to improve.

Confidence is not the absence of self-doubt; it is being able to live with it as your companion but not as your master. And remember even the most famous people throughout history-experienced self-doubt.

So if self-doubt is inevitable how do we deal with it? Simply follow the example of the greats and seek outside help.

It is not a sign of weakness to seek help because we, as a species, are not meant to work in isolation. We actually work better as part of a group, sharing ideas and problems are natural. This does not mean we look for help randomly but rather we should find someone we can trust and feel comfortable confiding in.

Finding a trusted advisor is a key element for building confidence, and of course finding the one who can best serve your confidence needs is very important. I really like the way that Paul McGee in his book "Self-Confidence" deals with finding the correct trusted advisor. He divides them into four categories each with their own strengths and weaknesses.

The trusted advisor.

1. The encourager. This is someone that believes in you and tells you and everyone else how good you are. When they are with you, they are very positive and energetic. However they may have unrealistic expectations, or have the necessary experience to help you achieve your goals.

2. The challenger. This is someone who will make you look at your thinking, motives and plans in an attempt to bring realistic expectations to the table. They will make you think more strategically, validate every decision with research and dispense with procrastination. However, their no nonsense approach may be de-motivating, and may not be appropriate when emotions are running high.

3. The coach. This is someone who will help you examine what it is you need to succeed. They will

provide structure, hold you accountable, and help provide clarity while remaining emotionally detached and rational. However, most coaches are a costly option and you may not get on because they are detached.

4. The confidant. This is someone you trust and who supplies you with emotional support. Because you know them you can be yourself and off-load all of your hopes and fears. However, they may not be the best-qualified person to help you as they may lack the relevant experience.

As you can see there is no one fix-it-all advisor. You really have to choose someone that suits the situation you need advice on. The challenger may be good if you are working through a business deal or idea, but would be totally the wrong person to talk to if you were feeling emotionally low.

Q: Who is the best type of person that I need to help me currently;

- The encourager.
- The challenger.
- The coach.
- The confidant.

Summary.

- Lack of confidence does have its benefits but none of them will aid personal growth.

- Real confidence is not based in bravado.

- Self-doubt is natural and if controlled, can be quite healthy as it can make us examine our talents and weaknesses.

- Asking for help is not a sign of weakness.

- Choose the trusted advisor that best suits your needs.

5 Building the foundation.

Identity.

I was at a cross-cultural conference recently were people from a variety of religious and cultural backgrounds shared their experiences. There was a great deal of open discussion, some of it uncomfortable at times, but the overall consensus was that many delegates's perceptions about other cultures were distorted and inaccurate.

"If I believe something to be true then it must be true" is an old saying that comes to mind. Our interpretation of the world around us is determined by our belief system, which in turn is tied up directly with our personal identity.

At this conference some delegates showed outward expressions of their identity by what they wore, others were more subtle and expressed themselves by the language that they used. What was very clear was the innate need for all the delegates to express their identity.

This need to find and express our identity is within us all. At the cross cultural conference there were some people who did not hold any religious belief yet attended every presentation, which outlined the fundamentals of the various faith systems. When talking to some of these individuals it soon became clear that they were seeking a religion they could join, a faith that would represent their identity.

There are some people that go through life like lost souls, looking for something, not really happy in their own skins. These are usually the ones without a definite identity and who are trying to find themselves.

In my early days of teaching I worked a lot with troubled teenagers. These were bright young people who came from dysfunctional families and therefore had identity issues. The lack of identity came because the family unit had provided no guidelines so they were looking elsewhere. Unfortunately, the major influence, and misplaced sense of identity, came from the paramilitary gangs in their own area.

The majority of these young people suffered as a consequence of the troubles in Northern Ireland. What is really interesting, though, is how many of these individuals reformed and turned to religion. This is not unusual nor should it be viewed with cynicism. These people make this change with real conviction and sincerity. They have traded a destructive identity with a more constructive one through religion. As one pastor said to me recently, "they have found themselves in God and that makes them happy"

To have a sense of identity we must feel we belong. As we go through life our identity will evolve according to our circumstances and the direction of our personal development. What we aligned our identity with, as a teenager may not be the same as today, although we will retain some reference to our past in an attempt to retain some of our individuality.

Billy Dixon

The diagram below shows the importance of identity in personal confidence.

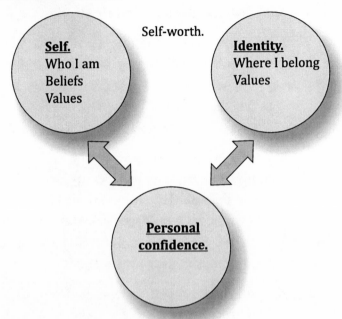

Identity is essential to our psychological well-being, it is the mirror we look at ourselves in the morning, it is what we present to the world, it is how we see the world and it is how the world sees us. Some would say without an identity we are no-one, I would disagree with this as I believe everyone is someone even if they are confused about who they are.

So where does our identity come from?

- Part of it is in our genes and is reflected in our personality, this we can do very little about, except understand it and manage it.

- Our family influences part of it. Mums, dads, brothers, sisters and all the extended family play a

42

part in forming our identity. However, if that family is dysfunctional, the individual may seek their identity somewhere else. Some of the young people I taught, came from unstable homes, found their identity within the street gangs of their area rather than in the family unit.

- Our friends influence part of it. Some experts would argue that our peers have a bigger influence on our identity than our families. I'm not sure about that, but I do know they definitely play an important role in defining us as individuals.

- Our culture influences part of it. We are all influenced at a very early age by where we live. Our belief system is often tailored via our parents, friends and teachings laid down by our culture. Mass media and access to the World Wide Web has diluted some cultures, but it has also helped nurture more extreme views and encouraged even greater divisions.

- Our belief system influences part of it. All of the above and our life-experiences form our beliefs, which shape the way we view the world around us and see ourselves.

- Our job, career, and position in life also play a part in our identity. Many occupations have their own specialist language, a dress code, standards of behaviour and specific working environments, which can create a strong sense of belonging and identity. Unemployment and retirement often cause identity problems, leaving individuals feeling empty and demoralised produced through a sense of not belonging.

- Our partner, husband, wife and children influence our identity. This unit can give an person a very strong sense of belonging and become a cornerstone of their identity. It can also cause a severe identity crisis should the unit split. However, a family split caused by a marriage breakdown has no psychological effect upon the children providing both parents have access to the children and provide a happy environment.

- Our hobbies and interests are often mirrored in our identity. The rock fan, the hiker, the antique collector, all reflect elements of their pastimes in their personal identity.

We all display our identity through:

- Our language.

- Our dress.

- Our behaviour.

- Our choice of space.

Almost every group, whether ethnic, faith based, sporting or business will separate themselves with the language they use, the clothes they wear, their rules of behaviour and where they meet. This gives their members a strong sense of belonging and identity. As individuals we all tend to display the signals that represent the group we represent and the status we hold within that group.

Understanding something about your identity is a real confidence booster. Take for example football supporters; their identity is closely allied to their team. They wear the team colours to show that this is the tribe they belong to. They mix with fellow supporters to watch a match or talk about the merits of the various players or the latest manager. This all gives them a sense of belonging, a sense of acceptance and a sense of well-being, all of which are great confidence boosters.

International sports teams are made up from the best players and athletes within the country. What is really interesting is that the majority of individuals turn up to the early training camps in their club kit. Their club represents their current identity and they feel safe, secure and confident in that environment and their kit represents that. The challenge that international managers face is not to take that club identity away but add an extra dimension to it, that gives that person an even stronger identity. If they fail to do this, there will be no team ethos, no team value system, and as a result the team will not bond.

Personal values.

The values we live our lives by are influenced by our personality, our strengths and weaknesses, and especially our belief system. How we establish and define these has given rise to many discussions and debates as well as numerous theories. Apart from telling us what they should be, few, if any, have been able to come up with a system that can tell us what our core values are.

Billy Dixon

Ask most individuals what values they hold dear in life and you will get the usual answers of: family, happiness, faith, health, honesty and so on. These are all good strong values, but burrow down into what they mean and some very interesting differences will start to surface.

Family for some may mean only mum, dad and the children; whereas for others it will be mum, dad, children and all the extended family. Family values may be based upon a strong worth ethic where the children are expected to contribute at an early age. On the other hand the children's education may be the priority and the parents will make great sacrifices to ensure they get that.

Happiness for some may be several holidays a year, for others it could be a good meal. What makes someone happy at a particular moment in time may change according to their mood or changing circumstances. Happiness is different for everyone, some are happy when they are moaning, others are happy when they are singing. Some are happy with their own company, others need a crowd. However we choose to define it there is no general standard that will suit us all.

The other thing to remember is that many of us do not know what our value is until we are faced with a particular circumstance. I witnessed this during the workers strike in Northern Ireland in the early seventies when businesses were forced to stop trading. This meant that many families were struggling to get the basics such as bread and milk. In order to feed their families some parents reverted to stealing, something they would never have considered under normal circumstances.

Some of us may not know what our value is until we are asked the question. Most people will give a negative answer if asked about tax, however, ask about the health service, education or the care of the elderly and where the funding should come from then the answers might be quite different.

Some core values are difficult to define but I suppose it really is a matter of conscience. It is how we decide we are going to live our lives in a reasonable stable and safe environment. However, when the element of unpredictability steps in, few of us really know what rules we would apply then. We might like to think we would react in a perceived correct manner but reality has a strange way of changing mind-sets.

There is one very simple fact that relates to personal core values. If you knowingly compromise or betray them then your self-respect and self-esteem suffer. There are fewer bigger confidence destroyers than self-deception and the betrayal of personal core values.

I must admit that I struggled to work out what my core values were. There were the obvious ones such as family, integrity, and fairness; but there was something missing. When I started to examine my motives for doing things I realized that because of my poor self-esteem that I needed to be acknowledged and praised for what I did. This need for recognition may not be classified as a core value according to the technical definitions, but it was a very powerful motivator and tended to drive much of what I did. However, what I was prepared to do to achieve recognition was determined by my core values.

47

Drivers are our motivators; core values are our conscience and both complement each other. It may be much easier to determine your drivers and then work out what rules you are prepared to adhere to in order to achieve these.

The following exercise is a very simple solution to establishing personal core values:

Write down one of your drivers and then what you are prepared to do to achieve it.

Drivers.	Core-values.
Power.	Integrity.
Money.	Family.
Fame.	Faith
Status.	Equality.
Recognition.	Sharing

Conflicting values.

Where some people struggle is when they are forced to work inside a group they cannot identify with or where their personal values conflict with that of the group.

A recently qualified young graduate in my hometown had been unable to get a job in the area of his expertise because of the economic recession. The only employment he could get was as a traffic warden, handing out parking tickets to illegally parked vehicles. The team he worked with were renowned as being predatory and unsympathetic, topping the league table for income generated from parking tickets.

The team's value set was completely at odds with this young man's, and yet he needed the job to survive financially. Rather than let this discourse depress him or change his personal values he worked according to his own values. He decided his job was to serve the public and only handed out tickets to those vehicle drivers parked in disabled parking spaces illegally, where inconsiderate parking caused inconvenience or was a danger to others. He gave directions to the elderly, the infirm and parents with young families to the most convenient parking spaces.

By creating his own value set within the group it allowed him to retain his own self-respect and identity yet allowed him to represent the team. This is a valid solution worth considering for those who find themselves in a similar situation but need the work.

5.1 Personality.

I have referred to personality on several occasions in this book and it is one question that I am asked regularly; does personality matter and can you change your own?

The current thinking in this area of research is that the largest portion of your personality is determined by your genes and the remainder by your belief system.

If this is the case then there are those who will argue that there is little we can do with the genetic part of our personality. In theory this is true, however, if we were able to determine what our personality traits are then we could at least manage them.

A young person, with a naturally aggressive trait, put in the wrong environment could turn into a violent thug – yet put into the correct environment could channel that aggression into something positive, like sport.

One of the best publications on personality is Daniel Nettle's book "Personality-what makes you the way you are?" Nettle divides personality into five categories and suggests that we can have traits in more than one. In his book you can do the "Big Five Personality test" which if done properly will give an indication of your personality type and traits.

As part of the confidence building exercise, it is always an advantage to have some idea about your personality traits. You will notice I say "some idea" as it is virtually impossible for any test to give a totally accurate reading of your personality, despite what some gurus would claim.

The following list of personality types with their traits are commonly used as a benchmark by many well respected therapists. Although they will not give you a detailed in-depth analysis of your personality, they are useful as a tool to access your general strengths and weaknesses.

There are five tables to work through over the next three pages including Neuroticism, Extroversion, Conscientiousness, Agreeableness and Openness.

5.1.1. Neuroticism: (worriers)	
Respond more to negative stimuli.	
Good at spotting risks and problems.	
Realistic.	
Avoid exposure to risks and danger.	
Nervous and anxious.	
Sensitive and innovative.	
Creative.	
Hard working	
Artistic.	
Academic.	
Thoughtful.	

5.1.2. Extroversion: (wanderers)	
Outgoing.	
Sociable.	
Positive.	
Enthusiastic.	
Risk takers.	
Need recognition.	
Easily bored.	
Thrill seekers.	
Unpredictable.	
Ambitious.	

5.1.3. Conscientiousness: (controllers)	
Disciplined.	
Make plans.	
Set goals.	
Not easily tempted.	
Efficient.	
Consistent.	
Like structure.	
Loyal.	
Don't like change.	
Like to be in control.	

5.1.4. Agreeableness: (empathizers)	
Thoughtful.	
Sensitive.	
Self-sacrificing.	
Understanding others.	
Put relationships first.	
Put others before themselves.	
Avoid conflict.	
Supportive.	
Slow to anger.	
Can be exploited.	

5.1.5. Openness: (poets)	
Imaginative.	
Creative.	
Eccentric.	
Erratic.	
Not realistic.	
Interesting.	
Romantic figure.	
Good with concepts and theories.	
Fascinating.	
Hard to live with.	

53

Personality Types.

Establishing your personality type is less important than understanding your traits. In each of the categories listed above, tick the traits that you believe are most representative of the person that you are. To get the most out of this exercise it is important to be as honest as possible. It may be also useful to ask someone you trust for their opinion in relation to the traits.

At the end of the exercise count the traits ticked in each section and the one with the largest number of ticks will give you some idea of your personality type.

Do not worry if you have ticks evenly spread over more than one category, it does not mean that you have multiple personalities, it just means that there is no one size fits all in personality testing.

It is interesting how such a simple exercise like this can be so revealing, it can throw up things that you did not realise about yourself or had just taken for granted. What makes it particularly useful is that it is a great starting point for working out your strengths and weaknesses.

5.2 *The key to success.*

The next practical step is one of the most useful and liberating exercises any individual can do. It is profound in its simplicity and yet is often misunderstood in its application.

Make a list of your strengths and weaknesses making sure to include your personality traits both positive and negative.

On every course I have ever attended that has included this exercise, the trainers have always instructed us to take our weaknesses and turn them into strengths. I believe that this method is fundamentally flawed as some of our weaknesses can damage our core strengths.

One of my core strengths is creativity and one of my core weaknesses is a poor eye for organisational detail. I have been told on numerous occasions that I must turn my detail weakness into a strength. When I tried to do as I was advised my creativity suffered, it was being stifled because I was trying to do something that was contrary to my natural ability.

I am not suggesting that we should not attempt to turn our weaknesses into strengths; we all have areas that we can improve. But there are certain weaknesses that should be left alone because to try to change them would only damage what we are good at.

As a result when advising others I ask them to make their list and then go through the following simple three step process.

5.2.1. Highlight your core strengths: these are the things you know you are really good at. They represent all that is good about you. You may be known for these skills. They may be a talent you are born with or an ability you have developed.

Then ask yourself a simple question; "what am I doing to make these core strengths stronger?" If you are doing nothing to develop your core strengths you are in danger of losing them. If you are in a competitive position, whether sport or commercially, good tactical brains will start by attacking your weaknesses and once they get you defending these they will then attack your strengths. If they can make you doubt a core strength your confidence and self esteem will drop.

5.2.2. Circle your core weaknesses: these are the things you can do nothing about, try and change these and you damage what you are good at.

You should now have a list with your core strengths highlighted and your core weaknesses circled. Take a moment to look at these because you have just admitted that you are good at some things and not good at others. This simple exercise in itself is liberating because most people are never as honest with themselves as this.

5.2.3. Turn the remaining weaknesses that are not circled

into strengths. Be sensible about this stage, don't try to change them all at once, prioritise and change one at a time.

This simple exercise has been completed in this manner by some of the most notable people in history. Successful people have all got one thing in common; and it has little to do with personality traits, mental ability or qualifications, I know these all help, but the real reason they are so successful is because:

> Successful people try to work only at what they are good at and work with others who can do the things they are not good at. In other words they work to their core strengths and work alongside other people who can complement them by covering their core weaknesses.

Read any success story and you will find this as the common theme, the majority of successful people did not do it on their own, they needed others. From Richard Branson to Anita Roddick, Margaret Thatcher to Ronald Reagan, Mother Teresa to Bob Geldof, they all needed other people. By focusing on your core strengths and working with others who can complement your core weaknesses, you can accomplish much more.

Time also needs to be taken at this stage to examine some of your beliefs as many have a direct effect upon your personality, strengths and weaknesses. To understand these gives you an element of control either through change or management.

6 Reflection.

The word "Therapist" is often associated with celebrity, the neurotic, the rich, the couch and, of course, looking into the past to explain current behaviour. Many regression therapies have been discredited and outlawed as they were proven to do more damage than good.

This is not to say that we should not examine our past to explain our behaviour. There have been some excellent results from highly researched therapies that are practiced by responsible clinical psychologists.

The problem with examining our personal history is that some will become so obsessed by the past that they can do nothing in the present. They can explain or even excuse their actions and reactions with events and experiences in their childhood.

Yes, our past has an affect on how we behave today and we should revisit some of our more challenging past experiences. However, we must not wallow in it, rather we should examine and learn from it then leave it.

6.1 The key to success.

Examine your belief system, talk to someone who is impartial and you can trust, be frank and open with them. What you believe may have been distorted somehow and may not even be the truth. The fact is if we believe a lie then it is the truth.

Here is a very simple but effective exercise to help establish some of your belief-systems.

Subject area	Belief	Why
Personal value		
I feel inferior to some people		
I find it hard to talk to strangers		
I don't like parties		
I don't like putting people out		
I useless at		
I'm just a mother		
I'm not that important		
I'm just used		
Politics		
Politicians		
Parties		
Voting		
Local councils		
Families		
Marriage		
Adoption		
Gay marriage		
Children		
Discipline		
Extended family		

Subject area	Belief	Why
Law and order		
Anti-social behaviour		
Crime		
Jails		
Punishment		
Capital punishment		
Music		
Classical		
Rock		
Pop		
Blues		
Hip-hop		

You will require several sheets of A4 paper ruled and headed as follows.

6.1.1. Subject area: choose any area of life; for example politics or religion or music and then sub-divide each subject area into themes that you might have an opinion on. (See examples above)

6.1.2. Belief: write down your belief or beliefs about that theme. (See example above)

For example:

Subject area	Belief	Why?
Anti social behaviour	It is worse now than ever	I see the young people shouting and misbehaving on the streets. I see evidence of vandalism. There are lots of hoodies in my area. It is on the news all the time.

6.1.3. Why: write down where you think that belief might have come from.

The chart above is only a guide for some of the subject areas and themes you might want to consider. Really you should include anything that you consider important in the makeup of your belief system.

Here are some other subject areas without themes that you might want to consider.

- **Education**
- **Health service**
- **Social services**
- **Taxation**
- **Immigration**
- **Health and fitness**

Beside each one of the themes write what your personal belief or opinion is about it.

Beside every belief or opinion write why you think this?

Once we have established the why then we can determine if the reason for that belief is founded on good reason or on misguided opinions.

- Q: are there any more young people on the streets than say twenty years ago?
- Q: are they causing trouble or is it simply a case of high jinks?
- Q; is it all the young people who are causing the vandalism, or a small minority?
- Q: is the vandalism worse than it was twenty years ago?

- Q: are they wearing their *hoodies* to hide their faces or is it simply fashion?
- Q: is the news coverage a true representation of society at large?

You can see what is happening here, just check your beliefs by asking some simple questions and see if you come to the same conclusions. It's amazing how many people have done this exercise and understood where their beliefs have come from.

By doing this with a trusted advisor you can then go on to change those beliefs that are damaging your personal confidence and self-esteem.

Your past can make you bitter or it can make you better and if used properly it can have real benefits.

6.2. Nostalgia.

We must not confuse examining our past to explain our attitudes, beliefs and behaviour with nostalgia.

For most people nostalgia is looking back at our past with warmth and fondness. We recall events in great detail and often refer to them as the "good old days".

There are those who claimed that being nostalgic was nothing but an unhealthy pre-occupation. However, new research reveals that the opposite is true.[6.1] [6.2]

It has been found that warm, happy nostalgic memories helped lift the mood of people who were sad or lonely by reminding them of happier times.

Nostalgic memories tend to centre around relationships where we are accepted and happy. They also tend to have a positive outcome, which gives us a sense of fulfilment. As a result our mood improves and we are in a better position to deal with the challenges of the present.

[6.1] Wilson, J. L. (2005) *Nostalgia - Santuary of Meaning,* Rosemont Publishing & Printing Corp.:Cranbury, NJ.

[6.2] Sprott, D. E. (2004) 'The power of reflection: an empirical examination of nostalgia advertising effects', *Journal of Advertising,* Wednesday, September 22 2004, All Business - A D&B Company (accessed: 11/12/2010 - http://allbusiness.com/marketing/).

Billy Dixon

I recall my past with great fondness: walking two miles across the fields with Sammy Porter to see Top of the Pops; the joker that was my mother; chasing girls with my mates, Walter and Ken; the fun I had with my students; my skydiving partners; teaching Aikido and my special dogs. Happy memories that make me smile and look at the now in a more positive light.

The conclusion of the research on nostalgia is that it fosters a sense of well-being and helps protect us against the psychological onslaughts of the future. These memories are especially detailed and vivid, we tend to nurture and protect them more than any others. They can help alleviate feelings of sadness, loneliness, unhappiness, frustration, failure, poor self-image, loss of confidence and mild depression.

However, it is very important to note that the research also concluded that nostalgia did not help people overcome severe depression although the researchers believe that it does help with the patient's self-image, but this has yet to be verified.[6.3]

So when you are feeling down, when your confidence has taken a knock, reflect upon the good old days. Go back to a time when there was fun and laughter, when you were on top of your game, when you were surrounded by people you liked or loved and where you know there is a positive outcome. You will find that your mood and confidence will improve and the challenges of now are dealt with in context.

[6.3] Routledge, C et al (2006) 'A blast from the past: The terror management function of nostalgia', *Journal of Experimental Social Psychology 44 (2008) 132-140*, Science Direct/Elsevier.

Also, remember this does not give us an excuse to live our lives retrospectively all of the time as this would be very unhealthy. It is simply that we can use nostalgia as a tool to help us with the now and to reaffirm an important part of our identity.

Hopefully, you should now have a greater understanding of your identity and the person that you are. With this basic foundation you are now in a better position to build real sustainable confidence.

Success.

Success is an important personal confidence builder, and continued success can develop sustainable personal confidence. It is very easy to be confident and enthusiastic when everything is going well, tasks become easier, moral is high, and there is a general feeling of well-being. However, if taken for granted and not managed properly, it can be destroyed very quickly when faced with setbacks or failures. We have all witnessed successful individuals and teams go into freefall when faced with a series of failures or poor results.

The thing to remember is that success can very rarely be guaranteed and is never permanent. Therefore, when we do enjoy a level of achievement we should try and learn as much as possible from it and, if possible, manage it in an attempt to sustain and build upon it.

There are those who would say, "If we are winning why change"? This is a very understandable attitude. However, it does not take into account the ever-changing environment that we live in, the improving quality of our competitors and the many other factors that are continuously evolving.

Success can only be measured against a series of elements over a particular period of time. The winning car in a formula one race from last season is not competitive this season. The business model that reaped large profits three years ago is now outdated and no longer appropriate.

Not only do we need to enjoy our success but we also need to learn and build upon it. Knowing all the ingredients that went into achieving it is a really good starting point. This can be done formally in an audit format or informally via open discussion and perhaps a combination of both. Whatever method is used, the reasons for the success should be listed, analysed and understood.

The following audit is only an example. Each audit needs to have the criteria that are specific to the individuals or teams operation.

You should always try to improve and change things when you are successful to maintain your competitive advantage for the next time.

What part does luck play?

I know that there are those who say we make our own luck and that success is all about planning, preparation and application. To some extent this is a valid argument, however, it does not take into account those unexpected events that can turn a deal, a game or the direction of

The success audit.							
Reasons for success:	Excellent.	V Good.	Good.	Fair.	Poor.	V Poor.	Improvements.
Planning.							
Preparation.							
Innovation.							
Application.							
Leadership.							
Management.							
Team.							
Commitment.							
Fit for purpose.							
Training.							
Communication.							
Marketing.							
Support.							
Networking.							
Customer care.							
Review and evaluation.							
Attitude.							
Luck.							
Other.							

someone's life.

Whether we want to admit it or not, luck does play a part in our successes. Yes, we can put ourselves into a position where we have the advantage, but how often have we seen the best team, the best person fail because of simple bad luck.

How much does luck play in success? In my opinion only a little bit, but it can still be the difference between winning and loosing. That is why we have to be honest and admit we were lucky to win and what form that luck took.

Learn from failure.

Everyone experiences failure during their lifetime. For some it is so traumatic that they just give up while others keep on trying until they succeed. Failure can have a negative effect on personal confidence if not managed properly, however, if dwelt with correctly it can clear the path towards achievement.

You have to understand how to loose before you know how to win.

To help you manage and understand the causes of the failure start by doing the success-audit and analyse in what areas you did well, what areas you did not do so well and what you could do to improve. This is a great way of getting things into perspective and preventing you from going into "lets beat me up" mode.

Make sure to include how much luck, or lack of it played a part in your failure, as this is something you could not have

Attitudinal decline.							
Signals:	Excellent.	V Good.	Good.	Fair.	Poor.	V Poor.	Improvements.
Withdrawal							
Isolation							
Secrecy							
Avoidance							
Fewer meetings							
Angry exchanges							
Ridicule							
Set easy targets							
Lack of commitment							
Low moral							
Blame others							
Neglect							
Denial							
Panic							
Bitching							
Discounting							
Easy payment deals							
Lack of respect							
Poor communication							
Negativity							
Low aspirations							
Initiative diminishes							
Not accountable							

predicated.

Attitudinal failure.

Some failure is caused by unfortunate circumstances or just bad luck. However, a large percentage is avoidable and is the result of poor attitude. If an individual is not in the correct frame of mind then failure is the most likely outcome and a further decline in confidence is inevitable.

To avoid such a spiral it is useful to be aware of the signs of attitudinal decline. The audit on the previous page has a list of the most obvious signals of a loosing attitude and if answered with honesty will flag up warning indicators that can then be dwelt with.

Attitudinal change requires awareness first and then a willingness to change. All this audit can do is help raise that awareness, the rest is up to the individual and what they are prepared to do to change.

Learn from failure, accept it, examine it and let it become the driver towards success.

Summary:

The foundation:

- Passion and purpose. Without these motivation is always going to be an issue.

- Work with people you can trust. Trying to build personal confidence on you own is virtually impossible.

- Personal identity is where you feel you belong whereas self is who you believe you are.

- Identity is reflected in an individual's language, dress, behaviour and choice of space.

- Understanding and managing your personality will also help establish and maintain your identity. You can do this by reaffirming your personality traits, establishing your strengths and weaknesses and understanding some of your belief system.

- Reflect a little on your belief system. Try and rationalise on the 'why' and 'how' accurate it is, then decide if you need to change.

- Remember that nostalgic memories can be used to create a positive mind-set.

- Success is a great personal confidence builder but never take it for granted. Learn from it and build upon it.

- Failure should be a great learning tool, use it as the foundation to work from and let it be your driver towards success.

- Attitudinal failure is a major cause of loosing, be aware of the signals and try to change them.

7. The fear of failure

Fear is a natural feeling that is part of our survival instinct, however, fear of failure is something that is programmed into an individuals mind in their informative years. Whether it is our parents, our peers, our teachers who have influenced these feelings; the bottom line is fear of failure is not an instinct, it is a mind-set.

How an individual thinks towards failure and success will affect what they will achieve in life. Many very talented and capable people have not achieved their full potential because they have been affected by a fear of failure.

Various clinical specialists have divided the mind-sets towards winning and loosing into four categories and although they may not be totally comprehensive, they do give very good signposts.

7.1. Low interest in winning and a high fear of failure.

Amanda is a bright articulate thirteen year old who, despite her obvious intelligence, struggles at school. In her end of term reports her teachers highlighted her obvious ability yet drew attention to her low levels of concentration and how she left so many tasks unfinished.

She lived in an area where there were lots of children and teenagers, yet seldom did she spend time with her own age group. Amanda preferred to play with the younger children where she was the leader and where she could win the competitive games.

This young teenager displayed all the characteristics of having a low interest in winning and a high fear of failure, and unless this mind-set was changed she would be restricted in her achievements in later life.

Typical characteristics of a low interest in winning and a high fear of failure are:

- Leaving jobs unfinished.

- Loosing interest easily.

- Competing against someone you know you can beat.

7.2.   Low interest in winning, low interest in failing.

As a lecturer, I met many academics who put a huge value on knowledge and dismissed the concept of competition. They saw their purpose as the development of their subject matter for the betterment of the intellect. Many, however, were in a race against other academics to be the first in their field or to be the most knowledgeable, and therein lies the irony.

These learned individuals may have a low interest in winning and a low interest in failing, but the researched based university system and the accolades associated with intellectual excellence have made their once cosy world a very competitive one.

Typical characteristics of a low interest in winning and a low interest in failing are:

- Indifference to competition.
- "Its only a game."

7.3. High interest in winning and a low fear of failure.

Some would say that this is the perfect mind-set. The individual, who relishes competition, but is not afraid to lose. They do not like losing, but when they do, they accept it graciously and try to learn from their defeat.

I did some work with a very talented racing car driver, who psychologically was one of the most balanced individuals I have ever met. He had a passion for driving and had set his goal to win a particular championship. His race preparation was always the same, and he entered every race with the intention of winning. Despite the pressures of the race meetings he always had time for his fans and was loved by his engineers and other team members.

No matter what the result of a race he would go over in his head; "What went well?" "What did not go so well?" and "What needs to be improved?" This cool calculated approach won him the very prestigious championship and I believe he will become one of the greats within his sport.

Typical characteristics of a high interest in winning and

a low fear of failure are:

- Love competition.

- Set goals.

- Not to be scared of losing.

- Take risks.

- Persistence and self motivated.

7.4.   High interest in winning and a high fear of failure.

When I was teaching I worked alongside a colleague who was an extremely talented athletic and he made sure everyone was aware of it. He was loud, brash and arrogant and seemed to enjoy humiliating others.

If he won a competition he would tell everyone how brilliant he was, but when he lost he always had an excuse. I suppose he could have been described as a bad winner and an even worse loser.

His athletic career did not last long despite his potential, and today he tells everyone, who will listen, how great he was and what he could have been.

I have met so many people from all walks of life like this, "talented failures" I would describe them as. People with great talent but restricted by their mind-set.

Typical characteristics of a high interest in winning and a high fear of failure are:

- Enjoy competition.

- Take personal responsibility for outcome.

- Failure causes self-doubt.

- Failure lowers self-esteem.

- Scared of taking risks.

- Not persistent.

- Can appear arrogant.

Whatever your mind-set, it does not make you a better or lesser person; it is just the way you are at this moment in time. However to maximise your potential, it is recommended that an individual adopts the "High interest in winning and a low fear of failure" mind-set as this is the one that is considered to be the most balanced.

You will notice that I say adopt, as a mind-set is something that we can all change. I was brought up in a rural part of Northern Ireland where politics and a firebrand version of religion were a large part of everyone's life. These teachings had a definite influence on my mind-set and that of all of my peers. As I become more informed through education, travel and sharing with others, I made conscious decisions to change my mind-sets towards certain aspects of my life.

I definitely was the person who took personal responsibility for everything that went wrong, and as a result my confidence and self-esteem suffered as a result. The real problem was, I didn't realise I was doing it. And herein lies the problem, "if you don't know you are doing something wrong how can you fix it"?

- The first stage of changing a mind-set is realisation. What mind-set do I have towards winning and loosing?

- The second stage is. Do I want to change it? If there is not the willingness to change then there can be no change.

- The third stage is. What do I have to do to change?

I like to keep everything as simple as possible and what worked well for me once I had made the decision to change was:

- Know what I want to achieve.

- Set short-term six-week goals.

- Review my progress at the end of every six weeks.

- Always ask three questions:

  a. What went well?

  b. What did not go so well?

  c. What needs to be done to improve?

The world stage is full of people who have changed their mind-sets. The war-maker turned peacemaker, the industrialist turned environmentalist and the wealthy turned philanthropist. It all comes down to a matter of realisation and willingness.

Summary:

- Fear is a natural instinct and reaction. However, handled wrongly it can destroy your ability to succeed.

- Your attitude to winning and losing is a mind-set that can be changed.

- Try and establish you own personal core values.

- Avoid compromising your core values as this will have a detrimental effect on your confidence and self esteem.

8 The building blocks.

Ask any group how many of them would consider themselves to be confident individuals and you would be amazed how few will answer 'yes'. In my experience, the majority of people do not consider themselves completely confident, they will feel confident in certain situations but not in others.

The fact is, no one is completely confident nor can we ever be completely confident. Complete confidence is just hype sold by the self-help industry.

You, I and the majority of people in the world have what is called "Focused Confidence" — something the majority of self-help books fail to acknowledge.

Focused Confidence

This is the technical term that suggests that we are all confident with things, situations and people that we are familiar with. In other words, we all live in a comfort zone of confidence. Take us out of that comfort zone and our confidence is challenged or leaves us completely.

To expand our focus of confidence we must step outside

our comfort zone and take on new challenges. As a lecturer I always encouraged my students to step outside their comfort zone, firstly to expand their zone of confidence and secondly to help them develop strategies and tactics to deal with new and challenging situations.

Every year I would take a group of students to do a charity sky-dive, definitely a large step outside of most people's comfort zone. I always found that the majority in the class liked the idea of jumping out of an airplane but very few actually took up the challenge. For those that actually did the jump, the change in their confidence and general attitude was always positive and often resulted in higher academic achievement.

One student who accepted the parachute jumping challenge was called Bill. Now Bill was underachieving and was not obtaining the grades I believed he was capable of. However, he had charm in bucket loads and made everyone he came in contact with smile.

We only discovered on the day of the jump that Bill had never flown before. So, the first time he was to go up in an airplane, he was also going to jump out of it.

At 1,000 feet, as the jumpmaster, I was watching the drop zone and calculating the run in direction for the jump, when I hear sobbing in the aircraft. It was Bill, he was sitting crying and ignoring the efforts of the other students to help. I asked him was he all right but he could not even answer and the sobbing just got louder.

When we reached our jump height of 3,000 feet, Bill had

cried that much the front of his red jump suit was totally darkened with tears. I asked him again if he was all right and this time he replied "I'm sorry, sir, but I can't do this, I can't jump". I told him to relax and he could come down in the plane with me.

The other four students jumped, while showing various levels of nervousness and bravado, leaving only Bill and myself in the aircraft. I asked if he wanted to jump or did he want to land in the plane? To my absolute surprise he said, "I'll give it a go, sir". He shuffled towards the exit on his bum, hung his feet out off the door and took up the perfect exit position, while all the time still crying.

I will never forget the small pale face looking at me, tears dripping off his chin, sitting in the aircraft's door at 3,000 feet. When I shouted "GO", he did the perfect exit, his parachute opened a few seconds later. I followed him out and landed in the field beside him, he was on his feet bouncing with excitement and adrenal, saying he wanted to do it again. So we duly obliged and put him on the next plane.

Two years later, Bill and two American skydivers won the freestyle, freefall championship of the world. Bill was a natural and was doing things in freefall within months that had taken me years to master. He just had a feel for the air.

We recently shared a commercial flight together and he said that one day had changed his life because it took him out of his comfort zone and made him look at challenges differently. After his skydiving success he went back to university, completed his studies and now this once under-achiever is the CEO of one of the largest pharmaceutical companies in the world.

Now, I am not suggesting we all need to be looking for challenges as extreme as Bills, but we all need to step outside our comfort zones to grow on a personal level. After all, if we are doing the same things the same way as we did last year, why should we expect things to turn out differently?

Not everyone will want to look for challenges and stretch themselves, as they have a degree of security and predictability living within their comfort zone. There is absolutely nothing wrong with this, but for those who want to develop, on a personal level, expanding the focus of their confidence is essential.

Below, you will find an exercise called "The Focused Confidence Audit". This will help you realise those areas in your life where you feel confident and the areas where you do not feel confident. From this you can then decide where you can extend yourself outside your comfort zone.

Focused confidence audit.

- Who are all the people who make you feel confident, relaxed and comfortable in their company? Now ask yourself why they make you feel like that?

- Who are the people who reduce your confidence and make you feel uneasy and tense in their company? Now ask yourself why they make you feel like that?

- What situations make you feel comfortable, confident and relaxed? Now ask yourself why they make you feel like that?

- What situations reduce your confidence and make you feel tense and uneasy? Now ask yourself why they make you feel like that?

- What places make you feel comfortable, confident and relaxed? Now ask yourself why they make you feel like that?

- What places reduce your confidence and make you feel uneasy and tense? Now ask yourself why they make you feel like that?

Personal confidence can be improved by challenging those people, places and situations that make you feel tense and uneasy. This will require you to step outside your comfort zone to face your discomfort and learning from the experience.

As a young man I had been written off educationally and I honestly believed I was stupid. When I finally got the qualifications to study in higher education I almost did not accept the offer to attend the Ulster Polytechnic. In my head I believed I was going into an environment where everyone was confident, intelligent and superior to me in every way.

In the first semester, I did everything possible not to get myself noticed by the lecturers or my fellow students. I let others answer questions during classes; I kept myself to myself at break times and in the evenings; and I attended none of the social functions organised by the students union.

Slowly I started to realise that my work and my opinions

were of an equal standard and in many cases at a higher standard than some of my peers. When I eventually started to talk to others on the campus I discovered that so many others felt inadequate and were struggling to find themselves. By Christmas, I had taken a few, but very important steps, into student life and had built up a circle of friends. I was starting to voice my opinions in lectures and my social life had improved dramatically.

By the end of the first year my grades were among the best in the class. I had joined several societies and sports teams and a group of us went to America to work over the summer months.

Little did I know at the time, but those first tentative steps into higher education really took me out of my comfort zone and challenged my self-belief and opinion of myself. When I look back at those days I think of some of the people in my hometown who had the talent but stayed in the safety of their environment and as a result never fulfilled their full potential.

I was lucky, I had a mother and a teacher who had faith in me. Both pushed me out of my comfort zone, others I know have not been so fortunate. This is why I am a great believer in seeking help from a trusted advisor if you do not have such support systems.

Stepping outside your comfort zone is a challenge; it can be painful, unsettling and downright uncomfortable. However, the potential benefits can be massive; it can improve self-belief, change perceptions, put things into perspective, broaden your horizons and improve your personal confidence.

8.1 Positive thinking can be dangerous.

The shelves are full of self-help books that promote and quite often insist upon the idea of positive thinking. We cannot live a fulfilled and full life unless we think positively. We cannot be successful unless we think positively.

Let us look at the facts. The human brain is not wired to be exclusively positive. Our brains are wired to be positive and negative. In fact, the brain responds to negative stimuli more than it does to positive stimuli.[8.1]

Throughout human history, our survival has depended upon us looking for dangers and threats. Our fight or flight response, housed in that little part of the brain known as the amygdala, is essentially negative and protects us by responding to anything it perceives as a threat.

Danger by its very nature is negative, and if we are programmed to look out for danger then it is obvious that thinking negatively is a natural instinct.

Where I get very frustrated is the unnatural emphasis that is put on positive thinking by some self-help gurus. I have witnessed entire teams, and organisations, paralysed by

---

[8.1] Cacioppo, J.T. et al.(2002) *Foundations in Social Neuroscience*, Massachusetts Institute of Technology: Cambridge p. 509

positive thinking where to say or act in a negative manner was paramount to treason.

This does not mean that I am an advocate of negative thinking. I just believe that we need to bring a little realism to the table.

Essentially there are three types of thinkers and to describe these I would like you to picture the following scene. Three individuals sitting in a cave back in the days when survival depended on the ability to hunt and gather.

8.1.1. The positive thinker.

This individual is extremely positive and psyches themselves up by saying, "I will go out here today and get something to eat, and I will survive". With no thought of the dangers they run out and a wild animal has them for lunch.

We all know people who are very positive and will not accept anything negative into their lives. This is fine in principal but not very realistic. It is inevitable that we will all encounter negative actions, comments and situations. If we are not prepared for this, then the results can be catastrophic.

8.1.2. The negative thinker.

This type of thinker sits in the cave, refusing to go out in case they get injured, or killed, complaining about how hungry they are and blaming everyone else for their predicament.

With little to offer this group of people moan their

way through life, make little or no contribution and blame everyone else for their situation. They generally feel sorry for themselves, expect to be supported by others and are very good de-motivators.

8.1.3. Positive attitude.

In the cave this person will be thinking, "if I go out of here I could get killed, yet I need something to eat. How do I make sure I don't get killed and how do I make sure I get something to eat?"

This individual thinks positive and negative. However when they think negative they are always searching for a positive solution.

The individual with a positive attitude is a true survivor, taking the best and worst case scenarios into consideration and planning for both.

I watched a GAA football team playing a match recently. This is a team that would have been known for their mental resilience and toughness, yet they seemed to give up and accept defeat easily, early in the game.

Several years before, they had appointed a new manager who was a big fan of positive thinking. All of his backroom team were chosen because they were positive thinkers and this theme was promoted throughout the camp.

Every training session was positive, every team talk was positive, everyone had to act positive and match preparation was based upon a positive outcome.

Billy Dixon

As the players' mental preparation was based solely upon positive thinking when things were going against them, during the match, they could not cope. In other words, when faced with a negative situation the players were not prepared mentally for adversity.

Had they been coached on positive attitude perhaps they would have been able to cope with when things were not favourable.

8.2 Optimism wins?

Optimism; defined as "A general disposition to expect the best in all things", has been claimed by some self appointed gurus to be an essential element of success.

Several of these so-called experts claim that optimism is essential to winning, long life, happiness and good health. This claim flies in the face of all the latest research and just pure common sense.

Optimism (the certainty of a positive outcome) should not be confused with positive attitude (a thought process that manifests internal strength in overcoming obstacles). Even a pessimist can have a positive attitude.

In his book "Personality", Daniel Nettle divides personality into five different types, the first of these being Neuroticism.

Neurotics, or worriers, respond more to negative stimuli and would be categorised as pessimistic in their outlook. However, they are also considered to be, sensitive, innovative, creative, hard working, artistic, academic and thoughtful. Their ability at spotting risks and problems, make them strong project leaders.

Nettle and his contemporaries also argue that personality

is largely genetic or inherited. So, being an optimist or a pessimist is just part of us, and does not inhibit our ability to be successful. Yet, having a positive attitude does have a direct effect on our chances of success.

The most frustrating thing about all of this is the way these self appointed experts write off the natural potential of large numbers of people because they are pessimists and then offer those same people the opportunity to buy their advice on how to become an optimist. This makes these positivistic gurus no better than the potion salesmen of the Wild-West.

So let us look at the facts. I would consider myself an optimist, someone who expects most things to turn out right. Has this made me more successful than my pessimistic contemporaries? Absolutely not! In fact, there are several who have reached the pinnacle of their careers, are happily married and are living fulfilled lives.

However, you will notice that I said "I expect most things to turn out right" not that "I expect everything to turn out right".

As with everything else in life, there are various degrees of optimism and pessimism.

Optimistic optimists are spoiled, perky underachievers who expect good things to happen at all times. When expectations are not met, they pout until someone gives them a treat. They are totally out of touch with reality and view non-perky others as inferior beings, completely unaware of how irritating their perkiness is to the rest of us.

Pessimistic optimists are wishful thinkers who want good things to happen but accept the imperfections of life. They hope for positive outcomes rather than working to make them happen and are not too surprised when things go wrong. But as with all optimists, they can do no better than break even or be disappointed with results.

Optimistic pessimists are realists who hope for the best but understand it rarely occurs. They're aware we live in a harsh world, thus they anticipate negative possibilities and adjust to circumstances.

Pessimistic pessimists are the meek who will inherit the earth. They comprehend the necessity of suffering and embrace it. They view life as a series of obstacles to be overcome.

Optimists either reach their high expectations or are disappointed -- pessimists either match the worst possibility or are pleasantly surprised.

Optimism is unreasonable wishful thinking. Intent is what makes a person succeed regardless of expectations, even when facing defeat. It is intent, not optimism, which makes a person invulnerable.

It is impossible to make people into positive thinkers if they are pessimistic by nature. They may pay lip service to the notion of positive thinking, adopt the actions and language, but inside they are still a pessimist. In fact, forcing them to adopt these positive traits can have a detrimental effect on their psychological well-being.

One of the best players in football (soccer) I have ever

worked with also happens to be a pessimist. In the game he would be considered to be the best tactically and technically in his position. His commitment on the field has earned him the respect of all who follow and play the game. And yet Frank (not his real name) always expects the worst.

So, no matter how much positive thinking I preached to Frank I was not going to change him as a person. In fact, I would probably lose him personally as he would see me as not being realistic.

The way to deal with Frank was to speak to him in his language but use it in a positive context.

Frank has recently been saying things like "I'm getting too old for this game" or "my injuries are catching up with me." My response has to acknowledge his feelings but must not reinforce them. My answer was; "well, here mate, you were still the fastest on the field." I did not tell him to think positive I simply acknowledged his ability thereby helping him maintain a positive attitude.

8.3 Developing potential.

I often get very frustrated with people who say to me, "well it's all right for you, you are good at something. Me, I'm good at nothing". What they are trying to say is that they do not have talent and that is the reason for their lack of success. They assume that because I present reasonably well on stage that I must be talented and that is what gives me the advantage over them.

The majority of us have probably been told by family members that everyone has a hidden talent. Well, I have been looking for mine for as long as I can remember, and you know what? I have never been able to find it. In fact, I have come to the conclusion that I have no talent.

Talent:

Talent is a gift that some people are born with. We either are a good singer or we are not, a good athletic or not, a good academic or not, and so on. However, it does not guarantee success. What an individual does with their talent will determine the level of success they achieve. We all know stories of talented individuals who have done nothing with the gift they possess.

Talent without confidence = failure.

Interestingly, the majority of successful people have no talent but have ability.

Ability:

Ability is something we learn how to do. No one is born a plumber, they have to serve years as an apprentice to learn how to become one. No one is born a doctor, it requires years of studying and supervised practice to become one. Most occupations that people are engaged in have to be learnt and are not reliant upon talent.

Knowing this certainly takes some of the excuses away for failure. Most of us can learn a skill, a discipline, or obtain the knowledge to become good at something. It simply requires effort, commitment and application.

Ability without confidence = failure.

Of course there are those born with an innate talent who have to develop an ability to make the most of it. In sport a young athlete with exceptional hand to eye coordination still has to learn how to play tennis, or soccer, or golf and so on. Their talent is dependent upon learning the rules and skills required for their chosen game.

There will also be those who have a talent but who are unaware of it. This may be for a number of reasons. Poor self-esteem may mean that the individual refuses to acknowledge their gift. Or the situation has never arisen where the talent has been called upon so it remains dormant.

Therefore, you do not need to have talent to be successful. It is simply a matter of finding something that interests you, developing the required skills and working hard to become good at it. Of course, there will be mistakes and disappointments along the way but then you will experience those no matter what you do.

Michelle, a student, considered herself a failure at the age of seventeen. She came from a family of high achievers and a lot was expected of her. After performing very poorly at the local grammar school she transferred to the neighbouring technical college.

It soon became clear that Michelle had been expected to follow in her parents' and brothers' footsteps to develop a career in medicine. Her future was mapped out, the relevant subjects chosen, the correct university decided upon. The only thing that was missing was that no one had ever bothered to ask Michelle if this was what she really wanted to do.

After just two weeks on a business studies foundation course, Michelle's life was changed. She developed a keen interest in retail marketing and excelled in her studies. She achieved exceptional grades throughout her stay at the technical college and was accepted on a marketing degree programme at Manchester University.

Today, Michelle has a hugely successful retail marketing company, which services some of the largest blue chip companies in the world. She has won numerous awards and has been named businesswoman of the year on several occasions.

Why has Michelle become so successful? Firstly, she

discovered a passion for the area of retail marketing. Secondly, she developed ability by studying and learning everything she could about the subject. And thirdly, she committed herself and focused on what she had to do to start her own business.

Like all of us, Michelle faced setbacks, failures, and periods of self-doubt on her journey, but she developed coping strategies to get her through the hard times.

We all have coping strategies when faced with adversity, some of us will run and hide, and hope everything will sort itself out, while others will go into denial. Some will become aggressive and others may decide to face it and try to deal with it.

Bookshelves and the web are abundant with publications telling us how to deal with adversity and how to build a better life for ourselves. Over the years I have read dozens of self-help books, the majority of which probably did me more damage than good. The sad truth is that many were based on dubious research at best or fraudulent research at worst. When asked today on what reading I would recommend? I tell people to start with "50 Great Myths of Popular Psychology – Shattering Widespread Misconceptions about Human Behavior" by Scott O. Lilienfeld *et al* and then decide what is appropriate.

8.4. *The Circle of Reinforcement.*

This very simple and practical tool was developed as a result of one man's tragic misfortune.

I coached an Aikido class in my local town for many years. One of my class, Patrick (not his real name), was a senior executive in the National Health Service and psychologically was one of the strongest individuals I have ever worked with.

Some time ago, Patrick was diagnosed with terminal cancer and given only nine months to live. Nine years later, he is still alive, his condition is still terminal and there is no chance of a cure, but as he said to his consultant "I accept the disease but I will not accept the time."

Rather than just accept his lot and sit back to wait for the inevitable, Patrick decided to take control of those parts of his life that he had some influence over. It is from his approach to his condition that triggered the idea of the circle of reinforcement.

We all have an anchor. This is an emotional expression that describes how we really think about ourselves. It may manifest itself in a word, or a phrase that we call ourselves in times of stress, when we make a mistake or when we are feeling low. Most of my life I believed I was stupid and if something went wrong or I made a mistake I would call myself a stupid ******.

Some people are lucky enough to have a positive anchor and are blessed with good self-esteem but for the majority of us we unfortunately beat ourselves up with a negative anchor.

Whether our anchor is negative or positive we all surround ourselves with things, people and attitude to reinforce that feeling. In Patrick's case his anchor is death and in the early stages things that reinforced his condition surrounded him.

- **Job:** Patrick could no longer work thereby reinforcing the fact he was dying.

- **Treatments:** Patrick has to have treatments administered to him in his home by a nurse every day. He was never sure what time the nurse was arriving and as long as he was sitting waiting he was reflecting on his condition thereby reinforcing the fact that he was dying.

- **Setbacks:** Patrick has had numerous setbacks each one reinforcing the fact he is dying.

- **Family and friends:** some of his relatives and friends came to visit Patrick and expressed their sympathy. Their conversations were full of negatives fed off his misfortune and reinforced the fact that he was dying.

If you look at the diagram below you will notice that all the arrows are pointing in towards the anchor obviously reinforcing Patrick's condition. In his own words, "if I had accepted and allowed this to continue I would be dead today".

The fact is, if we continually think in and feel sorry for ourselves we destroy our confidence and self-esteem. Start listening to other people and you will soon notice that the self-pitying and self-obsessed ones are also those with the lowest confidence and self-esteem.

Fact: people with low confidence and self-esteem think 'in'.

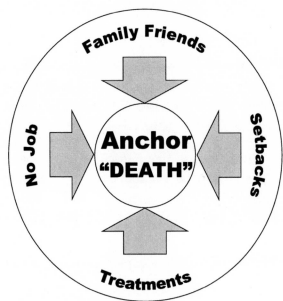

Fig. 8.1 Circle of reinforcement.

Patrick decided he needed to take positive action if he was to have any chance of getting some more time. The following is what has worked for him but at no time has he said that it will work for everyone with a terminal condition. He realises that there are times when no amount of positive action or attitude can prevent the inevitable.

- **Job:** He started a discussion group for people with terminal cancer in the local hospital. The meetings were originally just once a month, then once every two weeks and are now once every week. The model that Patrick developed is now being adopted throughout the UK and Ireland.

- **Treatments:** After a forceful discussion with the local health authorities, Patrick receives his treatments at eight thirty every morning leaving him the rest of the day free to do what he wants.

- **Family and friends:** Patrick made the decision to exclude all those people who de-energised and were pulling him down. The only people he now mixes with are positive energisers.

- **Setbacks:** Every time Patrick receives a setback he uses what he calls distraction therapy. He now speaks fluent Italian, has published a play which has been performed on stage, is writing a book on what it is like to live with terminal cancer and has become one of the world's leading experts on secret societies.

Now take a look at fig. 8.2 on (page 101) and you will notice that all the arrows are pointing out. By taking as much control of his life as possible and thinking outside the circle, Patrick believes he has extended his life.

People with healthy self-esteem and good levels of confidence think 'out'. They tend to focus on issues, people and projects external to themselves. It's interesting to note

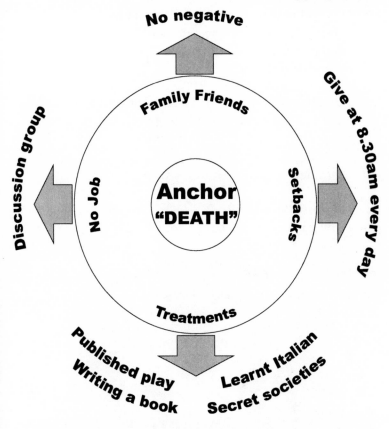

Fig. 8.2. People with healthy self-esteem and confidence think 'out'.

that one of the most effective ways of dealing with stress is to think out and help others.

So how can this help me and you? Can we apply it to our lives? The answer is a resounding 'yes' and it is remarkably simple.

8.4.1   Draw a large circle with a smaller circle in the middle.

101

8.4.2 If you know your anchor (what you really feel about yourself) put it into the small circle in the middle. If you do not know your anchor, do not worry this exercise will still work.

8.4.3 On the inside rim of the circle write all those things that you believe are preventing you from reaching your full potential. Some examples might be: age, attitude, experience, family, finance, health, lack of confidence, qualifications, where I live, and so on.

When I first did this my confidence and self-esteem were really low and my circle looked something like this.

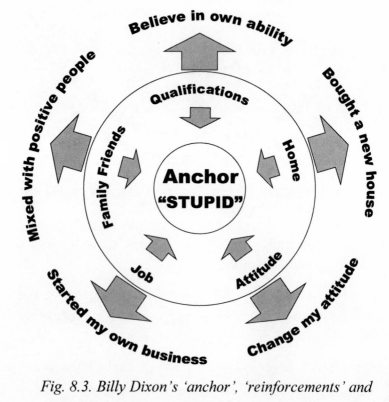

Fig. 8.3. Billy Dixon's 'anchor', 'reinforcements' and

My anchor was "stupid". I believed I was stupid after years of programming by the education system and myself.

My reinforces:

- **Attitude:** it was me against the world. I was self-effacing and self-critical and did not trust others.

- **Qualifications:** I felt I was under qualified but was not smart enough to enter the world of academia.

- **Job:** I taught many students who went on to build successful careers. I had not progressed in my career when they came visiting years later.

- **Home:** not being very practical my home was a DIY disaster area.

- **Family:** I could not afford the holidays or the lifestyle for my family that my peers seemed to be able to.

- **Friends and associates:** many of the people I mixed with thought the same way I did.

These are only some of the issues I was contending with at the time, but you will see that the arrows were all pointing in, keeping me firmly fixed to my anchor and maintaining my confidence at a very low level.

To be frank, I was just feeling sorry for myself because of my lack of progress and what I saw as the injustices of life. I believed I was a good teacher, so why was I not getting my rewards?

It was not until the sober realisation that my success

depended upon more than just my ability as a teacher and I started to break out of the circle of reinforcement that my life started to change.

- **Attitude:** I made a conscious effort to develop a positive attitude by keeping a log of how I felt every day and monitoring my self-talk language.

- **Qualifications:** I realised I was as well qualified as all the other teachers that I worked with, something I had never looked at before. Then I applied for a career break to allow me to study marketing psychology.

- **Job:** after twenty-two years of teaching I resigned from my position to develop my own business.

- **Home:** I employed experts to carry out any repairs on my home, thereby giving me more time to focus on my business and my family.

- **Family:** after several years in business and some hard saving I was eventually able to provide my family with some of the luxuries in life. However, what I soon discovered was the most valuable thing I could give to my children was quality time.

- **Friends:** I have kept all of my friends but always ensure that there is a healthy balance between the people who energise and those who do not.

Summary:

The building blocks.

- Personal confidence is focused on people, situations and things that we are familiar with. To improve our confidence we must step outside our comfort zone, meet new people, go to new places and take on new challenges.

- Our brains are wired to be negative and positive so the concept of positive thinking is misguided at best and destructive at worst. Work on developing a positive attitude, which allows you to think both negative and positive. However, if you think negative you have to come up with a positive conclusion.

- The concept that you have to be optimistic to win is a fallacy, it is more important to be realistic and to have a positive attitude.

- You do not need to have talent to be successful. However, everyone needs to develop ability. Decide what it is you want to do, learn how to do it and work at becoming good at it.

- What are the things that are preventing you from reaching your full potential and which of these can you change; in the short term, in the medium term and in the long term.

Remember that confident people think 'out' and away from themselves and people with little or no confidence think inwards.

9 Maintenance.

The energy audit.

When Patrick and I were discussing how he could try and manage certain aspects of his life, one issue kept surfacing. It was the people who come to visit him with the best intentions, yet left him emotionally drained.

The fact is some people thrive on other's misfortune and some folk are so negative they make everyone around them feel depressed. If we mix with these people on a regular basis, they will either pull us down, restrict our personal development, sow the seeds of doubt or, in Patrick's case, reinforced the fact he is dying.

From this experience the energy audit was developed and is something I use with every individual and team I work with.

- Using the diagram on page 107 make a list of everyone you know and work with. Categorise each individual either as an energiser or a de-energiser (some will appear on both as at times they energise and at other times they de-energise).

- Those that do not energise or de-energise put on the

ENERGY AUDIT	
ENERGISERS	**DE-ENERGISERS**

line in the centre as people who sit on the energising fence.

- Now highlight the people that you spend most of your time with.

- Is most of your time spent with energisers or de-energisers?

- Energisers make you feel better, boost your confidence, encourage you to succeed and generally create an atmosphere of positivity.

- De-energisers make you feel down, reduce your confidence, discourage you from trying anything new, create a stressful environment and generally create an atmosphere of negativity.

Who you mix with does have an effect on your general psychological welfare and we should strive to mix more with energisers than de-energisers.

Now, I am very aware that due to circumstances that it may not be possible to get away from the de-energisers, in which case you are going to have to get your positive energy from some other source.

9.1. Dealing with mistakes.

Dealing with mistakes is one area where people really struggle, especially those with low self-esteem. In the past, whenever I made a mistake I felt stupid, I was embarrassed, my self-esteem really suffered and I beat myself up physiologically. Then I made a remarkable discovery, most people I came in contact with did exactly the same.

When I started studying successful people I noticed that when they made mistakes they were not being pulled down to the same extent, so naturally the question arose, why not? One very famous football/soccer manager told me that how we deal with mistakes often determines how successful we will become.

When we make a mistake and realise what we have done, it is registered in the conscious brain. It is then passed on to be stored in the sub-conscious brain where, if not dwelt with properly, it will grow out of proportion — reducing our self-esteem and confidence. Somehow, we have to get the mistake from our sub-conscious brain back to our conscious brain so that we can deal with it rationally.[9.1a]

The solution is a remarkably simple one and has been tested and re-tested via numerous academic and psychological studies. It requires one sheet of paper, a pen or

[9.1a] Lazarus, R.S. (1999) *Stress and emotion: a new synthesis,* Springer Publishing Company: New York, p.103

pencil and then the following three step process.

9.1.1 **Write the mistake down.** This simple action transfers the mistake from the sub-conscious brain to the conscious brain making it easier to deal with. Writing something down also helps clarify what you have done and become more rational about the experience.

9.1.2 **Write down how the mistake made you feel emotionally.** Again this simple action helps you clarify how the mistake made you feel and transfers those emotional feelings from the sub-conscious brain to the conscious brain. It also helps put things into perspective, allowing you to be more rational about your reactions.

9.1.3 **Write down what you have learnt from your mistake**. A mistake is simply a lesson, but only if you do not make it again. This action registers the lesson on a conscious level and should help you stop making the same mistake again.

I have been using this exercise with clients for years, and what is really interesting is that people, who were making the same mistakes over and over again, are no longer making those mistakes.

Of course, there are times when it is not practical to take the time to sit down and write everything on a piece of paper. The sports field is a great example of this and yet every player will make mistakes during the game. Very few competitors have the mental capacity to ignore their mistakes. In fact, many react negatively and their game suffers accordingly. I have watched some exceptionally talented individuals go to pieces because they made a mistake.

So, are there any ways of dealing with mistakes in the heat of battle without sitting down and putting pen to paper?

Many sports stars use symbolism during a match. Some will reach down to pull up a few blades of grass. The grass represents the mistake and then they throw the mistake away. Others will clear their throat and spit their mistake away. I have seen golfers draw a line on the ground with a club and step over it, symbolically putting the mistake behind them.

Symbolism can be quite powerful, and can take many forms, but it has to be personal to you and something you can relate to. Use something that represents the mistake and then simply dispose of it.

9.2. *Dealing with negativity and stress.*

Much has been written about dealing with negativity and stress, unfortunately most of it is based on antidotal evidence. In a concerted effort throughout the world, neurological and psychological researchers are now publishing strong evidence on what are the most effective and ineffective ways of dealing with stress. [9.2a]

Solutions that do not work:

- **Punch something.** We have all heard of this one. Some companies actually provided employees with impact rooms, the idea being that the frustrated staff member could get rid of their anger by hitting something. A small minority did benefit from this. However, for the overwhelming majority it just increased their aggression.

- **Scream.** Sounds like a good idea, when overcome by frustration just scream or shout to get rid of the pressure. However, the research concluded that the benefits were short lived and the anxiety or stress

---

[9.2a] Kalat, J. W. (2008) *Introduction to Psychology*, Thomson-Wadsworth, Thomson Learning Inc.: Belmont. p.470.

returned within minutes.

- **Watch a funny film.** A nice thing to do which allows you to escape for an hour or so. However, that is all it allows you to do "escape" but does not solve the problem of negativity and stress.

- **Go to a party.** Just like watching a funny film this is just a short term solution and does not address the underlying issues.

- **Do a crossword puzzle.** Good for the brain but does not deal with the underlying issues.

- **Eat.** Comfort eating often exasperates the negativity and stress because of weight gain.

- **Do something creative**. Great thing to do but, apparently, does not reduce negativity and stress. I suppose Van Gough stands testament to this.

Solutions that do work:

The simple three-step process that we used for helping us deal with mistakes has also been shown to be one of the most effective ways of dealing with stress[9.2b] and is used by many practicing clinical psychologists to great effect.

9.2.1. Write the cause of your stress.

9.2.2. Write down how this stressful event is making you feel emotionally.

[9.2b] Kalat, 2008, p.470.

Billy Dixon

9.2.3. Write down what you have learnt or are learning from the experience both positive and negative.

- Helping others makes you think away from yourself and gets things in perspective. According to the experts[9.2d] this is one of the best reducers of stress.

- Listen to classical music[9.2e]. A great deal of research has gone into this one and the conclusion was that not just any old classical music would do, only Pachelbel and Vivaldi had the desired effect[9.2f].

- Sun exposure (minimum of 30mins continual exposure per week). Lack of sun exposure is a major cause of depression and stress, according to the experts[9.2g]. Long winter months with little sunshine are accompanied by an increase in the consumption of fat based comfort foods as people try to overcome the winter blues.

- Use humour to cope with stress. Laughter is the best medicine, or so research would conclude[9.2h]. Humour is a great tool to diffuse a tense situation. It can

9.2d Whealin, J.M. DeCarvalho, L.T. Vega, E.M. (2008) *Clinician's Guide to Treating Stress After War: Education and Coping Interventions for Veterans,* John Wiley and Son: New Jersey, p.57

9.2e Kahn, A.P. Meyer, D.H. (2006) *The Encyclopedia of Stress and Stress-related Diseases,* 2nd Ed. Facts On File, Inc: New York, p.250

9.2f Chafin, S. Roy, M, Christenfeld, N. (2004) 'Music can facilitate blood pressure recovery from stress', *British Journal of Health Psychology, (2004), 9 393-403,* The British Psychological Society: Leicester.

9.2g Kittleson, M.J. Denkmire, H. Rennegarbe, R. (2005) *The Truth About Fear and Depression,* Book Builders LLC: New York, p.123

9.2h Gostick, A. Christopher, S. (2008) *The Levity Effect: Why it Pays to Lighten Up,* John Wiley & Sons, Inc.: New Jersey, p.22

relieve the pressure when everything seems to be going wrong and it releases happy hormones into the bloodstream making us feel better.

- Get a dog. What was once a myth about man's best friend has now been verified by research[9.2i]. The companionship of a dog is now officially a stress buster and creates positivity in a person's life. Except when it chews your best shoes that is.

- Exercise. Often lambasted by the couch potato, exercise improves mood by releasing happy hormones into the bloodstream. It can also give an individual a more positive body image thereby improving self-esteem[9.2j].

Negativity is a natural part of life and practically everyone will experience it. How we handle it has an effect on our psychological well-being and will determine our level of confidence and self-esteem.

For most of us faced with a negative situation our natural reaction will be one of anger or disbelief or frustration. Nothing is wrong with any of these providing that we take control after this initial phase. Too many people do not get passed this stage and dwell upon the negativity rather than seek a solution.

Of course, there are situations in life where no amount of

[9.2i] ScienceDaily (1999) 'UCLA Researchers Find That AIDS Patients Who Own Pets Are Less Likely To Suffer From Depression', *Science News,* ScienceDaily.com: (Accessed 7th Jan. 2011: http://www.sciencedaily.com/releases/1999/05/990506065241.htm)
[9.2j]

positivity will solve the problem. In these situations sharing your concerns or worries with others is often the only option. After all we were not designed to live and work in isolation. As someone once said, "a problem shared is a problem halved".

I would offer a word of caution here — if you constantly appear to be the victim and your situation is not terminal, people around you will grow tired of your negativity and start to avoid you. Sympathy is only temporary and others will expect you to accept it with good grace and move on.

Self sabotage.

It is amazing the number of people who work hard to become successful in their particular field, achieve the rewards and recognition they have striven for and then self-destruct.

This kamikaze approach to success is really the result of poor self-esteem. The individual does want success but when they achieve it, sub-consciously they do not believe they deserve it, so they sabotage it.

Orla came from a very deprived area of Belfast. Like the majority of the people in the neighbourhood her family were all included in the long term unemployment figures. Just to put food on the table was a struggle and the whole situation was compounded by the troubles in Northern Ireland. Where Orla lived became one of the hot spots for paramilitary activity and violence was part of everyday living.

Through hard work and a determination to escape, Orla got the grades to study at a London university. Life as a student was not easy. With no financial support coming from her family she had to work at every opportunity to fund her studies. This gave her very little opportunity to socialise and mix with her fellow students, so life became all work and very little play.

In 1995, Orla passed her barrister exams and was given a position in one of the leading law firms in London. She quickly gained a formidable reputation and within a few years was invited to be a senior partner within the company.

At this stage everything in Orla's life seemed to be perfect, she was successful, well respected and wealthy. When she went home to see her family she was the toast of the neighbourhood. It was noticed by her mother, however, that Orla never seemed to hold down a steady personal relationship and when asked she often replied, "ah, sure I haven't met the right person yet".

It was in the late 1990s that things began to change. She started to be late for meetings, was depending heavily on her juniors to provide case research, there was a definite smell of alcohol on her breath throughout the day, her appearance became shoddy and she put on lots of weight.

Things came to a head when she appeared in court drunk and was threatened by the judge that if she did not leave she would be held in contempt of court. Luckily, her partners rallied round offering her counselling and time off to get things sorted out.

After a series of sessions with an excellent clinical-psychologist, it was established that Orla's path to self-destruction was caused by poor self-esteem. Subconsciously, she did not believe that she deserved to be successful. Perhaps it was being raised in an environment where people were deemed as worthless. She also believed that she was not deserving of the love of another person, which is why she could not hold down a steady relationship.

With help she rebuilt her confidence and self-esteem and, thankfully, was re-established as a senior partner in the firm one-year later. Today, she is happily married with three children, is a very successful and renowned barrister, and is chair of an organisation that funds a programme for underprivileged young people.

Spotting the signs of self-sabotage and doing something to counter them is a huge part of self-awareness and maintaining confidence.

Here are some of the most common areas:

- **Perfection**.

    There is nothing wrong with trying to seek perfection, however, we are all flawed and therefore perfection is all but impossible. Certain individuals expect to be perfect in everything they do and when they make a mistake or do not perform as well as they wanted, their confidence and self-esteem suffers.

    Winning individuals and teams accept they are

flawed and do not expect to be perfect, however, they always try to improve.

Accept that you are flawed and always try to improve rather than seek perfection.

• **Self-criticism.**

Do not beat yourself up too much when things do not go according to plan. It is all right to be self-critical now and again, but doing it all the time is unhealthy.

Become aware of your internal language, as it is a great indicator of the level of self-respect you feel about yourself.

Terms like "you stupid f-----", and "you useless b------", are great indicators of poor self esteem.

Consciously try to replace these negative words and phrases with a term such as "come on you can do better than that".

Or you can simply swear. Continuous swearing is inappropriate in most company and reflects an uncouth lack of discipline in the use of language. However, used appropriately it can also release tension and frustration.

Terms such as "I will succeed", "I will get this next promotion" or "I will score a goal" can be very damaging. This 'all-or-nothing' approach puts immense pressure on an individual to succeed, which is fine if they win. However, should they not achieve the levels they wanted then the self-criticism and the feeling of failure can become all-consuming.

I recently witnessed a head football coach give a team talk. He told his players "I will not accept us losing today", "I will not accept any excuses today if we lose", and "we will win this match today."

The team went out, gave it everything they had but lost the game. The effect of the coach's speech was much greater than the result. The team now believed they were losers because of what was said in the talk. They went into a run of bad form and lost their next six matches, putting them at the foot of the league. The coach was sacked and a new one was appointed.

This is a great example of how inflexibility can be so destructive, causing the lack of achievement to trigger self-criticism and self-doubt. It is much better to use a term such as "I have the ability to do this," or "I know what I have to do to win."

- **Take control.**

    Try to take control of your life and do not let others always drive your future.

Ben was a very talented teacher but felt frustrated and restricted by the risk averse and petty minded management team in the college. His teaching methods were creative, stimulating and brought the best out of his students, yet his head of department was putting more and more restrictions on him. He soon found himself speaking the same language as all the other demoralised teachers in the staff room. There was a general acceptance of helplessness and everyone was moaning but provided no solutions.

This drop in moral and motivation was also being transferred to the classrooms. Ben noticed the students were becoming complacent about attendance and work. Something had to be done, but he knew that there would be no leadership coming from the managers, as they were more concerned about college internal politics than the fate of the students.

Rather than become ineffective and resentful, Ben decided to take the initiative and work directly with the students, bypassing the management. He knew that his actions would probably be frowned upon, but his attitude was; "better to get something positive done and then ask for forgiveness, than to ask for permission and get nothing done."

He designed several assignments that not only empowered the students but also required them to work as a team, to make decisions, to take risks and to use their initiative. Despite a great deal of criticism and threats of disciplinary action from the management, Ben continued on his path with his students and ignored the opposition.

That year Ben's class won a national business competition for Further Education students; ran a very novel and successful fashion show, that resulted in them been asked by one of the large fashion houses to do the same for them; and, most importantly, all of the students got the necessary qualifications to continue on to higher education.

Rather than receive any recognition for his work, Ben found that things were being made more difficult for him. Everything came to a head, during a general inspection of his department, when three of his colleagues were deemed to be incompetent and he received a commendation.

No action was taken about the three and they continued in their teaching roles, destroying the educational aspirations of the young people they came in contact with. On the other hand — Ben found he was resented, seen as a threat and, consequently, given all the mundane work that stifled his creativity.

At this stage, Ben could have become demoralised, resentful and bitter. Instead, he re-examined his passion for teaching. His overriding drive had always been; "to make a positive difference to other peoples lives." Looking at it objectively, Ben realised that he could still do that outside of the educational system. Within a year he had left education and had started his own self-help/personal-development business, servicing both the private and public sectors.

Today, Ben is a celebrated public speaker and has travelled the world helping people to develop their personal belief and fulfil their potential. He still has an input into education, but on his terms.

- **Focus on the processes not the result.**

   Too many individuals and teams focus on the

result, the win or the goal and forget about how they are going to achieve it. To be successful you need to focus on the processes and the result will take care of itself.

Yes, you do need to know what you are trying to achieve, that is a given. However, unless the processes are carried out their can be no result.

Once you have set you goal, follow the processes and you will achieve it.

- **Take action.**

  One of the greatest contributors to failure, and destroyers of confidence, is procrastination. Unless you take action nothing can be achieved. Yet so many people with great ideas and with loads of talent fail because they did not take action.

  The fact is action leads to confidence, it is not confidence first then action.

- **Look for criticism.**

  Family and friends who have our best interests at heart surround most of us. They do not want to see us hurt emotionally, financially or physically, and will do their most to protect us.

  On the other hand, there may also be those close to us who are jealous and will try to sabotage everything we attempt.

Parties from both sides will usually offer advice and voice their opinions on our ideas or work. The rule here is simple — take their council with a huge pinch of salt, as they are too close and too emotionally involved to make rational comments.

It is much better to seek out an impartial advisor who will give impartial and rational feedback. You may not like or agree with what they say, but at least you will know their comments are unbiased.

If you do receive criticism do not allow yourself to be weighed down by it. Never ignore it, dwell on it or get defensive. Rather accept it, go away and think about it.

When weighing up criticism ask yourself a series of very simple questions:

- How valid was the comment?
- What was the person's motive for saying it?
- Do I agree with any of it?
- Would I do anything different?
- Should I seek further feedback?

Remember genuine criticism is a very valuable commodity as it can bring realism to the table and prevent you from making a huge misjudgement or mistake.

Setbacks are inevitable.

When Denise Lewis received her gold medal at the Sydney Olympics for the heptathlon, her smile hid the sacrifice and dedication that had gone into arriving at that point.

Like all great winners Denise had to overcome several major setbacks on her journey to success. On one occasion she injured her right knee so badly that she had to have surgery to repair the damage. What made this injury even more serious was that this was her take off leg in the jumping events. Rather than give up she came back and retrained her jumping technique to take off on the left leg instead.

She was making good progress and was climbing the rankings again when she seriously injured her left knee and again had to have surgery to repair the damage. At this stage many athletes would have given up, but not Denise. With the help of her coach and a change of technique Denise started taking off on her right leg again and the rest, as they say, is history.

Did Denise Lewis feel down and depressed about her injuries? Of course she did, however, she looked for positive solutions rather than excuses for quitting — and that is why she is an Olympic gold medal winner.

How we handle our setbacks will often determine our level of success. If Denise had fallen into the trap of self-pity and dwelt only on the negative without looking for a solution, then I doubt if any of us would ever have heard of her today.

Billy Dixon

Yes, it is healthy and normal to grieve when things go wrong. It is much worse to bottle things up and try to carry on as if nothing has happened. However, being the victim must not become a way of life as this is definitely unhealthy, plus others can only take it for so long before they become bored and start to avoid you.

Summary:

Maintenance.

- Try as far as humanly possible to mix with people who energise you and avoid those who de-energise, and pull you down.

- Remember that mistakes are inevitable, follow the three-step process to deal with them rather than beating yourself physiologically. You now have the tools to control your reaction to the mistake rather than have it control you.

- Everyone will experience negative and stressful situations in their life. How we react to these can often determine our levels of confidence and our psychological well-being. An element of control can be attained by using the very simple exercises

10   Faking confidence.

It is no coincidence that the majority of male national leaders all walk the same way, or that the majority of female leaders and stars all carry themselves in a similar fashion. The fact is, they will have been coached to project a confident image even if they feel uncomfortable and nervous.

Being nervous is natural and it can actually improve performance, if it is controlled. However, too many people allow nerves to control them, often freezing or going to pieces at crucial times. We all know the horror stories of the hot sweats, the dry mouth, being physically sick, not being able to string a sentence together, tears, tantrums and breakdowns all caused by the dreaded nerves.

It is also important to remember that acting and looking with confidence instils confidence in others. However, the opposite is also true; someone who appears anxious, nervous and uncertain, sets alarm bells ringing in other people's heads.

So what can we do to control our nerves and appear to be more confident at those important times? The answers to this question are much simpler than most people would believe and simply requires the individual to follow a pre-event routine.

I should point out the obvious at this stage, that before any meeting it is important to be well prepared. Know your facts, try to find out about the people you might be meeting and talking to, know the organisations history, and anticipate likely questions. We are fortunate today that so much information is available on the web, so there is little excuse for not being prepared.

The body and the mind are inextricability linked. Lack of confidence is often reflected in poor posture and submissive gestures whereas confidence is relaxed and open. We can all take some control and appear more confident if we develop a good pre-event routine.

The pre-event routine.

- **Posture.** Apart from whether we are male or female, this is one of the first things we notice about other people. There are postures that say aggression, aloofness, submission, fear and confidence. So make sure you make a good first impression with a relaxed upright posture where your head is up, the shoulders relaxed and your hands by your side.

- **Breathe.** When people get nervous they tend to shallow breathe, in other words they breathe into the top one third of their lungs only. This results in less oxygen getting into the body to feed the brain thereby causing a greater feeling of nervousness and sometimes causing panic attacks. It is important to learn to breath properly. Watch a child sleeping and you will notice that its chest does not raise and fall as it breathes but its tummy does. That's what we have to do, breathe from the diaphragm (the tummy) and not the chest. Sport stars, singers and actors are all taught this simple technique; place one hand on your chest and the other hand on your tummy, now breath in so that the only hand that raises and falls with your breath is the one on your tummy, the other one should not move. Now you are filling your lungs and your body and brain are being fed with oxygen making it easier for you to control your nerves. So before any potentially stressful situation, just take the time to breathe deep into your diaphragm.

- **Reconnect.** Stage fright, freezing, call it what you will, is a terrible experience. This is where the nervousness becomes so great that there is a disconnection between the brain and the body leaving the individual in a state of physical and mental limbo. To reconnect is a straight forward exercise and only requires a simple self-inflicted nip. The nip causes the body pain, which is registered by the brain thereby reconnecting the two. Another effective and very simple method is to juggle with an object, throwing it from one hand to another or even throwing it from one person to another.

- **Walk.** The walk can tell so much about a person's state of mind. Watch a winning team walk off a pitch and then compare their carriage to that of the loosing team. The moody teenage boy with his hands in his pockets, shoulders stooped and his head down, the teenage girl with her arms folded, shoulders stooped and her head down, both reflecting acute self-consciousness. A confident walk is relaxed, with hands swinging by the sides, head upright and shoulders back.

- **Smile.** When people get tense, nervous, anxious or angry they tense their jaw and facial muscles. Again this is a survival mechanism, the tense muscles are to help protect our faces and to prevent our jaw being broken in the event of an attack. However, it also gives out the message to others that we are uncomfortable and therefore not confident in this situation. Learn to relax your jaw and smile, this will ease the tension in your face and hey-presto you now look much more confidant.

- **Make eye contact.** We have all heard someone say that they did not trust someone because the other person could not look them in the eye. Eye contact acknowledges another person, it says, "I have noticed you and have acknowledged you." In western society it is also an indicator of personal confidence, so make sure to make eye contact with people, but please remember not to stare as this is perceived to be rude and threatening.

Learn from the likes of Barrack and Michelle Obama, Bill Clinton, Nelson Mandela and Cameron Diaz. Look at how relaxed they can appear when surrounded by the worlds press. The majority of these people will have a pre-event routine before they appear in public, allowing them to appear confident and in control.

If you practice faking confidence every day it will eventually become second nature and you will be able to do it without thinking. Interestingly, improving our posture and our walk, by smiling more and looking people in the eye, have been proven to improve self-esteem and personal confidence. It is the body's way of programming the brain.

Summary:

Faking confidence.

- Have a confident posture.
- Reduce nervousness by controlling our breathing.
- Find a way to reconnect our mind and body if we freeze.
- Walk in a relaxed confident manner.
- Smile.
- Make eye contact

11 Conclusion

When I started this book I never truly believed I would end up writing a conclusion. My internal belief system was telling me that my dyslexic brain would not allow me to transfer my thoughts into anything meaningful on paper. Yet here I am, almost finished.

Yes — it has been a struggle at times, but it has also been one of the most profound confidence building exercises I have ever done. I have been forced out of my comfort zone into an area, which in the past caused me a lot of emotional pain and made me feel stupid and worthless.

I would not have even started had it not been for the help of a man called George John Kingsnorth, who believed that what I had to say would be a help to others. With George's encouragement, guidance and honest feedback, I felt obliged to write, as I could not contemplate the thought of disappointing him.

So to write this book I had to make a decision to do it, I had to step outside my comfort zone, I needed the help of others and I had to take action. In other words, to have the confidence to write this book I had to apply the principals that are written about within this book. Now, having reached this stage I can say that my personal confidence has improved to such an extent that I have already planned and started a follow up book that will examine the area of physical confidence.

There are times and situations when you will need the help of others. Choose these people carefully, try and make sure that they will give you unbiased advice and direction rather than just telling you the things you want to hear. And remember — it is not a sign of weakness to ask for help, we are not meant to work and survive in isolation, we do need the help and advice of others and the good thing is — it is expected and natural.

This book would not have been written had I not discussed my ideas and fears with people that I trusted. Sometimes what they said was not what I wanted to hear, but that was part of the process that put things into perspective and gave me the confidence to continue.

Having personal confidence is not a given for anyone, it is something that has to be developed and maintained throughout an individuals life. It has to be built upon a solid foundation of personal understanding and awareness. This does not mean that we have to go on a journey of self-discovery where we analyse every little detail of our past. It is more about the acceptance of self; this is who I am, now what can I do to improve? Interestingly, the more we help others the more we discover about ourselves, so its not always reflection and navel gazing.

I have reflected on my past to try and explain my behaviour, but to be quite honest all I was doing was looking for excuses for my failures. When I focused my attentions on the young people I was teaching and tried to understand what made them tick, I found that my personal understanding and confidence was growing. I now believe that building personal confidence can and should be a shared experience.

Just because I talk and write about personal confidence does not mean that I can deal with or face every situation. The reality of life throws up situations that makes me have doubts and fears just like everyone else, however, the difference is I can now manage these much better.

The purpose of this book is to share with you the idea and tools that I have used over the years on myself and others, to help build and maintain personal confidence. But remember, confidence is not permanent; it is transient and often unpredictable. It can be affected by your mood, unforeseen circumstances, the weather and a host of other factors. All we can hope for is to have some element of control and understanding of it so at least we can manage it and stack the cards in our favour.

Firstly, we must be clear in our own heads what success means to us and know that we will have to work outside our comfort zone to start taking the first steps to achieving that success. This will mean clearing away all the unnecessary distractions in your life and establishing your passion, then your purpose and working on your focus.

Secondly, few of us can build anything without the help and guidance from others, and so it is with building personal confidence. With the help of a trusted advisor who will give honest feedback and support you will find this process much easier.

Thirdly, you must build a strong foundation otherwise any benefits will be short term. Understanding your personal identity and personality is a very good starting point as both of these define you — the person. From these you can then work out your strengths and weaknesses and decide upon the areas you may require guidance and help. This is always a good stage to do a little bit of reflection and conduct an honest appraisal of your belief system. With this greater understanding of self it is much easier to build and maintain personal confidence.

Fourthly, you have to put the structures in place to build personal confidence, and an important part of this is to understand that your potential is only limited by your willingness to learn and that developing ability is often more important than having raw talent. By using the circle of reinforcement you should be able to establish what is preventing you from reaching your full potential and then decide how you can change that.

It is important to keep your feet firmly planted on the ground at this stage as life has a nasty habit of coming up with a few surprises. Positive attitude prepares us to deal with both the positive and negative and does not hide away from reality. And remember being optimistic is not an essential element of personal confidence or being successful, being realistic is much more important.

Fifthly, there is no point in having a strong foundation, building a great structure and not maintaining them. Because personal confidence is being continuously exposed to the demands of everyday life it needs to be maintained. Trying to reduce your contact with energy sapping individuals and mixing with uplifting people is always a good starting point. Of course, you will make mistakes and face stressful events along the way but if you learn to deal with these properly they will make you stronger and more confident. The signals of self-sabotage are fairly obvious and you should be always on the look-out for them, if you have people around you that you can trust, they can also help you spot them.

Lastly, remember that how others perceive you may not reflect on how you feel. There are people who are full of confidence but don't look it and others who have no confidence and appear to be in total control. By taking on the persona of a confident individual, this is the one area that you can change almost immediately. Simply by adopting a relaxed confidant posture and walk, breathing properly, smiling and making eye contact, others will think you are brimming with confidence.

The thing is; everyone can improve their personal confidence if the will is there. It does require commitment and honesty but even the smallest improvement can reap huge benefits and rewards.

The choice is yours!

A novel by
ERROL BADER

Geocache (Paperback Book Thriller)

High in the Austrian Alps a solo pilot flies his high tech aircraft into a cloud filled canyon. A driving snow storm doesn't prevent a computer specialist leaving his car to walk into the Black Forest. Guided by satellite navigation both are drawn to an appointment they dare not miss.

A tragic accident above the Denver skyline puts the head of the Global Geocache Society into a coma triggering a deadly game across Europe as Victoria Kavanagh, his Chief of Security, races to find a rare donor.

Alerted by an Interpol Code Purple warning, Inspector Sean Mason gives chase to a predator, only to cross paths with Victoria. Can she be trusted or is she the one he is pursuing?

About the author of 'Geocache':

Errol Bader lives in Denver, Colorado with his wife Judith. He served as a White House Advance Man during the early Reagan years. He is a partner in USAERO LLC, the regional distributor for several aircraft manufacturers in the south western United States. Mr. Bader is cofounder of Aviation Mentors, advising owners of high performance aircraft and is a prolific airman holding many pilot ratings

Hidden (Paperback Book Science Fiction)

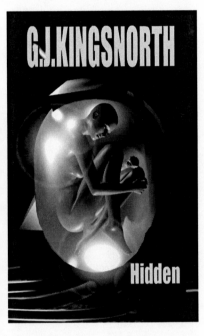

Imagine, if your world was controlled by computers, everything you wanted was automatically ordered by a computer. Your shower temperature, the food at breakfast, and the clothes on your back are all prepared by a computer. Even your education is dictated by a computer. Now imagine, that if you were to lose your job, everything would be gone, you would be outcast and prey to the preachers. If you were forced to leave the safety of your home, life could end on a whim of some corporate opportunists. What if the only thing that could save you were the images flooding into your mind? What if there was a message hidden within your thoughts that could save the world? What would you do?

About the author of 'Hidden':

George John Kingsnorth has been living in Northern Ireland for the past 26 years. For most of his career he has worked in television. For the past 7 years he has been a lecturer in Creative Media Production but continues to produce dramas and documentaries. George's first contributed to a series of books for Friend's of Ed before turning to write novels. 'Hidden' is George's second novel. He has also published the novel Geocache by Errol Bader. Also in post-production is George's second low-budget digital feature film 'Monty's Quest'. His early film 'Fiddler's Walk' can be purchased here on Amazon.

For more information visit
www.gullionmedia.co.uk

Lightning Source UK Ltd.
Milton Keynes UK

176985UK00001B/64/P